MASTER GUIDES

GENERAL EDITOR: JAMES GIBSON

JANE AUSTEN	*Emma* Norman Page
	Sense and Sensibility Judy Simons
	Persuasion Judy Simons
	Pride and Prejudice Raymond Wilson
	Mansfield Park Richard Wirdnam
SAMUEL BECKETT	*Waiting for Godot* Jennifer Birkett
WILLIAM BLAKE	*Songs of Innocence and Songs of Experience* Alan Tomlinson
ROBERT BOLT	*A Man for All Seasons* Leonard Smith
CHARLOTTE BRONTË	*Jane Eyre* Robert Miles
EMILY BRONTË	*Wuthering Heights* Hilda D. Spear
JOHN BUNYAN	*The Pilgrim's Progress* Beatrice Batson
GEOFFREY CHAUCER	*The Miller's Tale* Michael Alexander
	The Pardoner's Tale Geoffrey Lester
	The Wife of Bath's Tale Nicholas Marsh
	The Knight's Tale Anne Samson
	The Prologue to the Canterbury Tales Nigel Thomas and Richard Swan
JOSEPH CONRAD	*The Secret Agent* Andrew Mayne
CHARLES DICKENS	*Bleak House* Dennis Butts
	Great Expectations Dennis Butts
	Hard Times Norman Page
GEORGE ELIOT	*Middlemarch* Graham Handley
	Silas Marner Graham Handley
	The Mill on the Floss Helen Wheeler
T. S. ELIOT	*Murder in the Cathedral* Paul Lapworth
	Selected Poems Andrew Swarbrick
HENRY FIELDING	*Joseph Andrews* Trevor Johnson
E. M. FORSTER	*A Passage to India* Hilda D. Spear
	Howards End Ian Milligan
WILLIAM GOLDING	*The Spire* Rosemary Sumner
	Lord of the Flies Raymond Wilson
OLIVER GOLDSMITH	*She Stoops to Conquer* Paul Ranger
THOMAS HARDY	*The Mayor of Casterbridge* Ray Evans
	Tess of the d'Urbervilles James Gibson
	Far from the Madding Crowd Colin Temblett-Wood
BEN JONSON	*Volpone* Michael Stout
JOHN KEATS	*Selected Poems* John Garrett
RUDYARD KIPLING	*Kim* Leonée Ormond
PHILIP LARKIN	*The Less Deceived* and *The Whitsun Weddings* Andrew Swarbrick

MACMILLAN MASTER GUIDES

D.H. LAWRENCE   *Sons and Lovers* R. P. Draper

HARPER LEE   *To Kill a Mockingbird* Jean Armstrong

LAURIE LEE   *Cider with Rosie* Brian Tarbitt

GERARD MANLEY HOPKINS   *Selected Poems* R. J. C. Watt

CHRISTOPHER MARLOWE   *Doctor Faustus* David A. Male

THE METAPHYSICAL POETS   Joan van Emden

THOMAS MIDDLETON and   *The Changeling* Tony Bromham
  WILLIAM ROWLEY

ARTHUR MILLER   *The Crucible* Leonard Smith
                                          Death of a Salesman Peter Spalding

GEORGE ORWELL   *Animal Farm* Jean Armstrong

WILLIAM SHAKESPEARE   *Richard II* Charles Barber
                                          Othello Tony Bromham
                                          Hamlet Jean Brooks
                                          King Lear Francis Casey
                                          Henry V Peter Davison
                                          The Winter's Tale Diana Devlin
                                          Julius Caesar David Elloway
                                          Macbeth David Elloway
                                          The Merchant of Venice A. M. Kinghorn
                                          Measure for Measure Mark Lilly
                                          Henry IV Part 1 Helen Morris
                                          Romeo and Juliet Helen Morris
                                          A Midsummer Night's Dream
                                            Kenneth Pickering
                                          The Tempest Kenneth Pickering
                                          Coriolanus Gordon Williams
                                          Antony and Cleopatra Martin Wine
                                          Twelfth Night R. P. Draper

GEORGE BERNARD SHAW   *St Joan* Leonée Ormond

RICHARD SHERIDAN   *The School for Scandal* Paul Ranger
                                          The Rivals Jeremy Rowe

ALFRED TENNYSON   *In Memoriam* Richard Gill

EDWARD THOMAS   *Selected Poems* Gerald Roberts

ANTHONY TROLLOPE   *Barchester Towers* K. M. Newton

JOHN WEBSTER   *The White Devil* and *The Duchess of Malfi*
                                            David A. Male

VIRGINIA WOOLF   *To the Lighthouse* John Mepham
                                          Mrs Dalloway Julian Pattison

WILLIAM WORDSWORTH   *The Prelude Books I and II* Helen Wheeler

MACMILLAN MASTER GUIDES

WUTHERING HEIGHTS

BY EMILY BRONTË

HILDA D. SPEAR

MACMILLAN

First published 1985 by
THE MACMILLAN PRESS LTD
Houndmills, Basingstoke, Hampshire RG21 2XS
and London
Companies and representatives
throughout the world

ISBN 0–333–37286–7

A catalogue record for this book is available
from the British Library.

Printed in Hong Kong

Reprinted 1985, 1990, 1992

CONTENTS

To Walter

GENERAL EDITOR'S PREFACE

The aim of the Macmillan Master Guides is to help you to appreciate the book you are studying by providing information about it and by suggesting ways of reading and thinking about it which will lead to a fuller understanding. The section on the writer's life and background has been designed to illustrate those aspects of the writer's life which have influenced the work, and to place it in its personal and literary context. The summaries and critical commentary are of special importance in that each brief summary of the action is followed by an examination of the significant critical points. The space which might have been given to repetitive explanatory notes has been devoted to a detailed analysis of the kind of passage which might confront you in an examination. Literary criticism is concerned with both the broader aspects of the work being studied and with its detail. The ideas which meet us in reading a great work of literature, and their relevance to us today, are an essential part of our study, and our Guides look at the thought of their subject in some detail. But just as essential is the craft with which the writer has constructed his work of art, and this is considered under several technical headings – characterisation, language, style and stagecraft.

The authors of these Guides are all teachers and writers of wide experience, and they have chosen to write about books they admire and know well in the belief that they can communicate their admiration to you. But you yourself must read and know intimately the book you are studying. No one can do that for you. You should see this book as a lamp-post. Use it to shed light, not to lean against. If you know your text and know what it is saying about life, and how it says it, then you will enjoy it, and there is no better way of passing an examination in literature.

JAMES GIBSON

ACKNOWLEDGEMENTS

I should like to thank the staff of Dundee University Library for their ready assistance in various ways and the Dundee University Computing Centre. Thanks are also due to Mrs Moira Anthony, who typed much of this book.

Cover illustration: *A Heath Scene: Sun after Storm* by John Crome, courtesy of the National Gallery of Ireland.

H. D. S.

INTRODUCTION:
ON READING A NOVEL

When we read a novel – any novel – what do we expect from it? Is our first purpose to be informed, to be educated, to receive a moral, a social or a political lesson? It should not be: novels are meant to be enjoyed – enjoy them! The very worst way to read a novel for the first time is to read with pen in hand laboriously taking notes as you go; but notice those words 'for the first time': any novel worth reading is worth reading twice – or three times – or again and again and again! No one can read a novel for you; someone may tell you the story but this is merely the skeleton, which the novelist fleshes out; the novel itself is much more than mere story. A quick first reading will help you to find your way about a novel but it will not have told you all about it. This introduction suggests some lines of thought for you to follow on your second and subsequent readings.

Who narrates the story? Is it told in the first person, the 'I' being the subject of the tale? Or is it perhaps in the third person, an omniscient narrator observing objectively the actions and thoughts of all the protagonists? Or is it more subtle than either of these simple methods? Are there several tellers, looking at the story from their own differing viewpoints, or telling different parts of the story? Is the main narrator an auditor too, who receives the story from one or more other narrators? Or is it difficult to decide who is telling the story, as it seems to be happening in the minds of the characters themselves? The method of narration has always exercised novelists, for on it depends the understanding and varying sympathies of the reader. A reminiscent first person story starts off with certain presuppositions – at least the protagonist survives and is able to tell the tale. On the other hand, the all-knowing third person narrator may predispose us to like or dislike particular characters; we may even feel that our sympathies are being manipulated.

From what point of view do we see the events of the novel? The straightforward first person narrator will tell the story from his own point of view; even if he attempts to show us other points of view they will be sifted through his own and we shall receive an essentially subjective account. The third person narration, from an impartial outside observer, generally purports to be objective; as soon as the narration is complicated, however, by the use of narrators with some sort of identity within the novel, then we must take into account narrative fallibility. The author may deliberately choose to have an unreliable or dishonest or naïve narrator; or perhaps one or more of the narrators will not have access to full information; on the other hand, a number of different subjective accounts of the same incident may give the reader an objective view. Certainly the narrative mode allows of wide variety and perhaps the only golden rule here is, 'Never confuse the narrator with the author'.

We can move on from discussion of the narrative method to consider the use of time in the novel. Even if there is no obvious exploitation of time as a narrative device we cannot avoid at least some thoughts on its significance. When was the novel written? If it was written fifty, or a hundred or two hundred years ago we must remember the differences that scientific and technological advances have made to our lives today, the differences in cleanliness, in household convenience, in leisure activities, in travel and communication; we must remember the differences in social, moral and religious attitudes and in family life. We shall also have to come to terms with the vocabulary and the prose style of an older novel. An historical novel may compound our problems, for we may be observing events of hundreds or thousands of years ago, interpreted through the understanding of an author from an age that is already past.

There are, however, other aspects of the novelist's use of time which we need to consider as we read. The simplest of these is that we may have to cope, in a few hours' reading, with the events of many years and adjust, in minutes, our response to slowly altering circumstances and gradual changes in character. More complicated are the deliberate time-shifts which the novelist makes in order to achieve particular effects: the flashback, the flashforward, the events narrated in reverse order, the events narrated more than once and at different points in the novel. Observe these as you read and ask yourself what the author achieves by playing with time in such ways.

Then there is the question of place. Where is the action of the novel set? Is it in some distant, exotic, foreign land that most of us will never see? Is it in the country? In the town? Is it so unfamiliar that it warrants several pages of description? Or is it familiar enough to need none? How essential to the plot is the setting? Does it give atmosphere to the novel? Or is it entirely insignificant, referred to hardly at all? The sense of place may well reinforce themes within the novel, or different characters may be associated with different places, the aspects of which reflect the characters themselves.

Of course, you will think about the characters as you read their story.

You will decide who is the hero (if there is a hero) and who is the heroine (if there is a heroine) and even who is the villain (if there is a villain); but how are these characters portrayed? Are they cardboard figures, lacking solidity? Are they caricatures, with only one feature of the characters emphasised? Are they mere reflectors, throwing light on other characters? Are they functional, fulfilling a particular but limited role? Or do they seem to be real people, reacting differently according to the circumstances, showing various aspects of their character, changing, growing, gaining our human sympathy and understanding? A good novel will probably have most if not all of these types of characters; those we respond to most readily are the ones who seem to be real but, as in life, there will be many characters who are seen briefly, superficially, who play their part in the plot and disappear from the scene; without them the novel would be poorer.

When Polonius asked Hamlet what he was reading, the reply was 'Words, words, words'. A novel is composed of words and ultimately its success depends on the choice of words, the use of language and the style for, skilfully couched in telling phrases, the dullest story may blossom, whilst the most exciting incidents may appear dull and insipid if they are recounted in flat tones and commonplace clichés. Observe how your author uses language. Is there a variety of style – formal? Colloquial? Poetic? Are there recurrent words and phrases? Realistic pictures which become images and symbols? Catchwords? Motifs? Repetitions? References? Quotations? Allusions? Is there dialogue? Do the characters speak in their own special idiom? Are we given the thoughts in their minds? Perhaps the very fact that we had not noticed the peculiarities of the language on a first reading demonstrates the skill of the author. However, that a technique is unobtrusive does not mean that it is insignificant and the better critics we become, the more we shall observe not only *what* is said but *how* it is said.

Perhaps the final needful question is, 'How do we become better critics? Have courage! Many of us have asked ourselves this in our time. First, *believe in yourself*. Read the novel through quickly, then read it again more slowly, giving thought to some of the questions outlined above. Only after this stage should you turn to the critics. You may then find that some of your own ideas about the book have been corroborated and this may suggest that you are working on the right lines. You may also find that other ideas you have had are in disagreement with the critic you are reading. Accept that you may be wrong but do not be afraid to suspect that the critic may be wrong. Go back to the text; it is the final arbiter; does it appear to support your argument or the critic's argument? Never try to defend an indefensible position. If you cannot prove your contention, give in gracefully; however, if you still feel you are proved right, do not allow yourself to be bullied by the printed word. Any teacher worth his (or her) salt learns a lot from students; every critic is vulnerable. Enjoy your novel-reading and go on reading more novels. You may well find that in the process you have yourself become a critic.

1 EMILY BRONTË: LIFE AND BACKGROUND

Emily Brontë was born on 30 July 1818 in the village of Thornton some miles to the west of Bradford in Yorkshire, where her father, Patrick, was curate. She was the fifth of six children, all brilliantly gifted, though the two oldest girls, Maria and Elizabeth, were to die in childhood and the only boy, Branwell, was to dissipate his talents and die with all his bright promise come to nothing. Charlotte, the third child, and Anne, the youngest, like Emily, became, novelists and poets and, like her, died too soon.

On 20 April 1820, when Anne was scarcely three months old, the family moved to the little moorland parish of Haworth to the north and west of Thornton, where Patrick Brontë had been appointed to a perpetual curacy. The parsonage at Haworth was Emily's home for the rest of her life. Less than a year after the move Mrs Brontë was taken ill; she died from cancer in September 1821. Thus the six children were left motherless; Maria the eldest was only seven; Anne was not yet two. Their aunt, Elizabeth Branwell, had already joined the household to help nurse her sick sister; she remained to care for the children and to run their home.

The early education of the girls was taken on by Aunt Branwell whilst Patrick Brontë himself tutored his young son. When Maria was nine years old, however, she and Elizabeth were sent away to school, first to Crofton Hall, near Wakefield, and then, in July 1824, to a school more within their father's means, the School for Daughters of Poorer Clergymen at Cowan Bridge near Tunstall. Charlotte joined them there in August and Emily in November. It appears that the school was disastrously badly run and the children neglected, if not physically ill-treated. The following year, 1825, first Maria and then Elizabeth came home to die and Charlotte and Emily left the school for good in June. Cowan Bridge School has been forever castigated through Charlotte's vividly recalled memories of it in *Jane Eyre*, which should be read in order to get some view of the horrors of the school system in the north of England during the early decades of the nineteenth century.

The four remaining children were now thrown back on their own resources. Their education continued at home but they were alone for much of the time. Living in an isolated community, they were even more isolated by their own particular circumstances. Children of the parsonage, they belonged neither to the upper-class society of the region nor to the local rustic folk. Thus, deprived of fellowship in real life, they created a world of their imagination. Their immediate stimulus was a box of twelve wooden soldiers given to Branwell in 1826. Around these soldiers the children wove an extensive and intricate drama, telling stories and acting plays based on the fictional land of Angria which was ambiguously peopled by the twelve wooden soldiers, representing historical and contemporary figures who were, simultaneously, the children themselves; so whilst Charlotte and Branwell took on the personae of the Duke of Wellington and Napoleon Bonaparte and re-enacted their battles through their representational wooden soldiers, Emily and Anne were more pacific heroes – the Arctic explorers, Edward Parry and John Ross. For the next few years their fictional world was developed, though the two younger girls never fully participated in the Angrian adventures. When Charlotte was once more sent to school in January 1831, Emily and Anne took the initiative and began to invent their own fictions centred on the imaginary island of Gondal.

None of the prose stories of Gondal is extant, though a few notes remain. For us today the Gondal saga is known mainly through the poems, which represent the emotional high-points of the whole chronicle. Emily and Anne lived so intensely within their own created world that the mood and tone of the Gondal poems reflect the inner turmoil of their own imaginative life, though the actual adventures of the inhabitants of Gondal, as far as we are able to deduce them, bear no relation to the lives of the two girls. Emily's love for the Yorkshire moors which were home for her is apparent in the Gondal landscape, for it is that of the countryside around Haworth. The wildness of the moorland, the aspects of untamed nature that exist side by side with the romantic peace and beauty of misty hills and bright summer days were also significant features of Gondal; they are present too in *Wuthering Heights* where the weather and the landscape have a profound influence upon the course of the plot.

These years at home with Anne were perhaps the happiest of Emily's life; the death of her mother and two elder sisters were sufficiently in the past for their memories to become dim (she had hardly known her mother); the misery and disgrace of her brother Branwell's excesses which were to cast a shadow on family life were not yet apparent. She was able to roam the moors, to read, to write, to draw and generally to give free rein to her imaginative life, but it was not to last. Charlotte had finished school at Roe Head in 1832 and three years later, in July 1835, she returned there as an assistant teacher and with her went Emily, as a pupil. Away from her home and her beloved moors, Emily languished. Her homesickness became so acute that after less than three months she left the school and her place was taken by Anne.

Now seventeen, Emily stayed at home and helped her aunt and 'Tabby', the sole household servant, in the kitchen and with other household chores. However, Mr. Brontë's circumstances were not such that, were he to die, his daughters would be provided for; it was necessary that they should be able to earn their living. Thus, in autumn 1837, Emily again left home, this time to become an assistant teacher at Law Hill School, near Halifax; though it is not certain how long she remained there, it appears probable that she returned home after about six months. She was certainly not happy there and again poetry served as an emotional outlet, her spiritual desolation being played out vicariously through her Gondal poetry:

> Sleep brings no joy to me,
> Remembrance never dies;
> My soul is given to misery
> And lives in sighs.   (See Hatfield edition, p.54)

After she left Law Hill Emily remained at home for the next few years whilst Charlotte and Anne took a series of posts as governesses and Branwell failed in one job after another.

In 1841 Charlotte conceived the plan of going to a finishing school in Brussels in order better to prepare herself to run a school of her own. Encouraged and financed by their aunt Branwell, both Charlotte and Emily went to Brussels in February 1842 to study at the Pensionnat Heger. They were pleased to be together and progressed well in their studies. Whilst there Emily developed her musical gifts; she already derived great pleasure from playing the piano and at the Hegers she was given skilled tuition. The original six-month stay was extended; the two Brontë girls remained in the school over the summer holiday period and started the new term in September. They now became both pupils and teachers, Charlotte teaching English and Emily music in exchange for their own lessons in French and German. At the end of October, however, their aunt was taken seriously ill and before they were able to get home she had died. They returned to England early in November, Emily never to go back to Brussels.

Now that their aunt was dead, it was necessary for one of the girls to take over the household. Thus Emily, never happier than when she was at Haworth, jumped at the opportunity to stay at home. Anne was still in a situation as governess at Thorp Green Hall near York and she arranged for Branwell to return there with her after Christmas as tutor to the son of the house. Charlotte went again to Brussels, drawn there by her growing hopeless love for her teacher, Monsieur Heger. Alone at home, Emily attended to household matters and cared for the various animals, in particular her own beloved dog, Keeper. The old servant, Tabby, who had retired some years earlier, returned to help a little with the chores and to give Emily company.

Catastrophes now began to crowd in upon the parsonage family: Charlotte remained in Brussels for a full year, returning to Haworth, lovesick and unhappy, in January 1844; the following year Anne resigned from her position at Thorp Green Hall and a month later Branwell was dismissed, accused of conducting an intrigue with Mrs Robinson, the mother of his pupil; meanwhile the Reverend Patrick Brontë was slowly going blind. During all this time Emily had never ceased to write poetry; in February 1844 she had begun to transcribe her poems into two notebooks, one for Gondal poems and one for other poems. She continued, at least partly, to live in her own imagined Gondal world and, though it could no longer satisfy Anne, it enabled Emily to face the trials around her with some degree of equanimity.

It was in the autumn of 1845 that Charlotte chanced to see and read one of Emily's manuscript books of poems and became convinced that they should be published. (Charlotte recounts the incident in the biographical notice of her two sisters which prefaced the 1850 edition of *Wuthering Heights* and *Agnes Grey*.) Emily was distressed and angry at Charlotte's intrusion into her private world and would not at first countenance publication; she yielded to persuasion, however, and work on preparation for a volume of the poems of all three sisters began. Emily and Anne each contributed twenty-one poems and Charlotte twenty. They were reluctant to use their own names – three unknown sisters from a Yorkshire parsonage appeared to them unlikely to claim public attention and they believed that the adoption of masculine-sounding names would allow the book a more propitious launching. Thus, in May 1846, *Poems by Currer, Ellis and Acton Bell* was published. Though the book, and especially Emily's poems, received very favourable reviews, it did not sell well. However, publication appeared to stimulate the three sisters and they began to explore the possibility of publishing 'a work of fiction, consisting of three distinct and unconnected tales'. (Letter from Charlotte, 6 April 1846, to the publisher of their poems, Aylott and Jones. Quoted in full by Gérin, p.187). These three 'tales' were Charlotte's *The Professor*, Anne's *Agnes Grey* and Emily's *Wuthering Heights*.

The Professor was not, in fact, published during its author's lifetime but Charlotte wrote and published *Jane Eyre* before *Wuthering Heights* and *Agnes Grey* were finally published in December 1847. They were again presented under the Brontës' masculine pseudonyms, for although Charlotte and Anne were now ready to declare their identities, Emily refused to allow her own name to be disclosed. Just as she had found imaginative release in the Gondal adventures, she seemed able to retreat from her own personality in the assumed identity of Ellis Bell. The character of Shirley in Charlotte's novel of that name (1849) was partly modelled on Emily; in the novel Shirley assumes the role of Captain Keeldar and feels more able to face the world; in just the same way Emily found the role of Ellis Bell a more comfortable public image than her own person. In 1848 Anne's second novel, *The Tenant of Wildfell Hall*, was published; it was swiftly followed by Branwell's death in September of that year. At least some of the themes of *The Tenant of Wildfell Hall* had been inspired by Branwell's dissolute life; he had become increasingly dissipated, drinking heavily and becoming completely addicted to opium. His sisters and father had to endure all his bouts of wildness and depression and it is not surprising that Charlotte, who had once been closest to him, despaired of helping him and abandoned him to his fate. Emily, however, tried to sustain him and until the end continued to have hope. He had hardly been ill, at least not more ill than normal, and his sudden death came as a shock to the whole family.

Branwell was buried on 28 September. At the funeral Emily caught a cold which went swiftly to her lungs; she never went out again. She would not accept medical help, however, rejecting bodily ills as some sort of moral weakness. Charlotte's letters of this period show how adamant Emily was that she was not sick enough to see a doctor. When Charlotte wrote to a homoeopath for advice he sent a prescription which Emily refused to take. It was only on the day of her death that she at last agreed to see the family doctor, Dr Wheelhouse; he was sent for but before he arrived she was dead. His certificate stated as cause of death, 'Consumption – 2 months' duration'. In her *Life of Charlotte Brontë* the novelist Mrs Gaskell (1810-65) tells how Emily's faithful bulldog, Keeper, went to her funeral service and when he came home 'lay down at Emily's chamber-door and howled pitifully for many days' (end of Chapter 16).

When Emily left Thornton, the place of her birth, she was still not two years old; for the rest of her life Haworth Parsonage and the surrounding moors were her home. Though she went away to various schools for brief periods, even travelling as far as Brussels, her spiritual home was always Haworth, where she returned, drawn as to a magnet. At least some aspects of Catherine Earnshaw's upbringing coincided with that of Emily and when, in Chapter 9 of *Wuthering Heights* she tells Nelly Dean that she once dreamt she was in heaven, she expresses sentiments that could well have been Emily's:

...heaven did not seem to be my home; and I broke my heart with weeping to come back to earth; and the angels were so angry that they flung me out, into the middle of the heath on the top of Wuthering Heights, where I woke sobbing for joy.

Less than ten years after Emily's death Mrs Gaskell described the approach to the village of Haworth from the nearby town of Keighley, climbing upward all the way. The village must then have been much as Emily knew it, sitting bleakly on a moorland hillside 'with a background of dun and purple moors, rising and sweeping away yet higher than the church, which is built at the very summit of the long narrow street' (Chapter 1). The parsonage stood above the church and looked across to the church tower and down towards the crowded graveyard; beyond the parsonage were the open moors, with their grandeur, their freedom and their solitude. These moors, which Emily knew so well, became the setting for *Wuthering Heights*. Several of the houses in the neighbourhood have been said to be the originals of Wuthering Heights and Thrushcross Grange; it is probable that Emily took certain features of houses she knew and allowed her imagination to play with them. Top Withins, high on the moor above Haworth, is generally assumed to be the site of Wuthering Heights, though both Law Hill School and the nearby High Sunderland Hall probably contributed to the descriptions of the Heights in the novel. Similarly, Ponden Hall, close to the River Worth and about four miles due west of Haworth, appears to have suggested some aspects of Thrushcross Grange but is by no means the Grange itself.

Unlike her sisters, Emily did not write her own experiences into her novel and neither Cowan Bridge nor the Pensionnat Heger have any significance in the plot of *Wuthering Heights*, though the history of Law Hill before it became a school undoubtedly provided the seeds for the story of Heathcliff. It is not necessary, however, to search for sources, for the novel is a great work of the imagination and should be appreciated as such.

2 SUMMARIES
AND
CRITICAL COMMENTARY

For the sake of clarity throughout the rest of this book, except in quotations, 'Catherine' and 'Cathy' are used to designate respectively the members of the older and younger generations.

Chapters 1 and 2

Summary

The novel begins with Lockwood relating the story of his first visit to Wuthering Heights in 1801. He has a good eye for detail and provides a vivid description of the outside of the house, the family sitting-room and Heathcliff. His encounter with the dogs produces an unease in the reader's mind which is not completely dispelled by the more sociable conclusion of the visit. When, despite the coolness of his reception the previous day, Lockwood returns to Wuthering Heights the following afternoon, he meets the younger Cathy and Hareton Earnshaw. Since no one bothers to introduce him to anyone it is only after a series of blunders that he learns the identity of these two. He is treated with extreme incivility and when he realises that night and snow have come on during his visit he asks to be guided back to Thrushcross Grange. His request is refused so, seizing a lantern, he rushes out alone, whereupon Joseph sets the dogs on him. He is finally rescued and taken inside again by Zillah, the housekeeper.

Commentary

As the novel proceeds we shall realise that Emily Brontë has used the narrative device of beginning the story *in medias res* i.e. in the middle. At this early point, however, it has every appearance of being a straightforward first person narration in diary form with Lockwood and Heathcliff as the main protagonists. These first two chapters have been used to set the scene for us and to introduce us to some of the main characters. Already the contrast between Wuthering Heights and Thrushcross Grange has been established, the former full of warmth and life with its 'immense fire' and 'table, laid for a plentiful evening meal', the latter cold, lonely and resistant to change. Yet we are puzzled by the inmates of the Heights and by the atmosphere of scarcely subdued animosity between them. The undercurrent of violence surfaces in the two incidents with the dogs; it is a prominent theme throughout the novel and is frequently associated with dogs.

Notice, too, how our minds are subtly prepared for the theme of the supernatural by the introduction of such words as 'magically', 'beneficent fairy', 'little witch', 'ghost' and by Cathy's assertion of her abilities in 'the Black Art'.

Chapter 3

Summary

Zillah smuggles Lockwood upstairs into a room which was not normally used; there he settles for the night in a bed situated beside a window and within a panelled cupboard. Before going to sleep he looks through the books lying on the window ledge and reads a kind of diary written some twenty-five years previously by Catherine Earnshaw. When he finally falls asleep he has a series of terrifying nightmares, in the last of which, unable to open the window, he breaks the pane and finds his fingers seized by the ghostly hand of a child. Terrified, and unable to release his hand, he rubs the child's wrist across the broken window-pane until the blood runs down and soaks the bed-clothes. He then snatches his hand inside but the ghost will not go away; he cries out in terror and Heathcliff enters the room. The ensuing scene is almost as fearful as the nightmare, for Lockwood sees Heathcliff, overcome with passion and anguish, throw open the window and cry out to the ghostly child. Next morning Lockwood returns to Thrushcross Grange.

Commentary

The first interpolated narration is here introduced and placed within Lockwood's narrative by the simple device of his finding and reading Catherine's diary from 'some quarter of a century back'. This gives us a completely different perspective of the story as we view the boy Heathcliff beaten, bullied and ill-treated and are drawn into Catherine's sympathy for him. The events which follow, whether real or imaginary, are seminal to the whole book. Lockwood's nightmare raises a dead Catherine Earnshaw, whom we have not yet met in the flesh; her ghostly appearance and words, however, will be recalled in Chapter 15 when, dying, she suggests that Heathcliff will have forgotten her in twenty years. This is, too, the first mention of the window in Catherine's bedroom at Wuthering Heights, where so much of the significant action of the book takes place.

Chapter 4

Summary

Lockwood's curiosity has been aroused by the events at Wuthering Heights and he asks his housekeeper to tell him something of Heathcliff's history. Thus, Nelly launches into her story, beginning with the arrival at the Heights of Heathcliff as a small waif, under the greatcoat of old Mr Earnshaw. Nelly explains that her mother had nursed Hindley Earnshaw and that she, Nelly, had lived with the family doing various odd jobs. Though she had disliked Heathcliff at first, she found him a very patient, uncomplaining child. She observes, however, that he brought trouble to the Earnshaw family from the beginning.

Commentary

Here, the chronological tale begins and Nelly's narrative takes us back in time to the year 1771, when Catherine is six, Hindley fourteen and Heathcliff is first brought to Wuthering Heights. Throughout the novel, references to the ages of the characters or to occasional dates enable us to trace very accurately the chronology of the whole story. The method of multiple narration is extended further in this chapter, though it is still within the framework of Lockwood's narrative. Nelly Dean now tells the story and we see the incidents and characters not through the outside and objective viewpoint of a stranger but through the eyes of one who has been familiar with all the events she is describing. This enables Lockwood, and through him the reader, to gain a new insight into life at Wuthering Heights. Any sense of the strange or unusual is lulled by the commonplace of a story told beside the fire on a winter's night with a passive listener and a narrator quietly sewing as she speaks.

The novel is greatly enriched by the wealth of dialogue, for both Lockwood and Nelly reproduce the spoken words of the protagonists themselves. We might also notice here the colourful turns of phrase which Nelly uses in her own narration with similes and metaphors drawn from the everyday life around her: 'Rough as a saw-edge', 'hard as whinstone', 'uncomplaining as a lamb'.

Chapter 5

Summary

During the years which follow Heathcliff's arrival at Wuthering Heights he and Catherine become very close to each other; her greatest punishment is to be separated from him and he is always more willing to fall in with her plans than with those of anyone else. There is constant strife in the household and at last Mr. Earnshaw is persuaded by the curate to send Hindley away to college. This does not bring peace, however, for both

Joseph's moralising and Catherine's high spirits cause trouble. Old Mr Earnshaw becomes more and more feeble until, in October 1777, he dies as he sleeps in his chair beside the fire.

Commentary

This short chapter carries the story swiftly forward over several years. It is a feature of this novel that the pace varies: a chapter may contain the events of a few hours or a few years.

Chapter 6

Summary

Hindley returns home for the funeral, together with Frances his wife, whom he has married secretly. He now takes over the household and banishes first Joseph and Nelly and then Heathcliff to the servants' quarters in the back-kitchen. He refuses to allow the curate to continue with Heathcliff's education and forces the lad to work as a farm-hand. One Sunday evening when Catherine and Heathcliff have been sent from the sitting-room, they disappear from the house. In the middle of the night Heathcliff returns and tells Nelly what has happened: it appears that the two had escaped from the house and gone to look at the Linton family through the windows of Thrushcross Grange. There they saw Edgar and Isabella quarrelling over a little dog but their laughter at this foolishness resulted in the Linton's bulldog being set on them. Catherine was seized by the ankle and after this both she and Heathcliff were taken into the house, the latter swearing loudly. When Catherine was finally recognised, the Lintons were horrified and tried to put matters right by bathing her ankle and making a fuss of her. Heathcliff, however, was thrown out of the house because of his foul language and as he now explains he has had to return to Wuthering Heights without Catherine.

Commentary

Again the narrative perspective changes as Heathcliff briefly takes over the story and we see the incident at Thrushcross Grange through his eyes whilst Nelly listens and interpolates the occasional comment. The reader has had a preview of some of the events in this chapter through Catherine's diary in Chapter 3; there she had described both the misery of Sunday evenings and also the harsh treatment meted out by Hindley to Heathcliff.

We should notice that once more a window – this time the window of Thrushcross Grange – is a focal point of the story. Throughout the novel windows are separators; here the window initially separates Catherine and Heathcliff from the Lintons but by the end of the chapter it separates Catherine and Heathcliff from each other; they are never to be truly happy together again.

Chapter 7

Summary

Catherine remains at Thrushcross Grange for five weeks and when she returns home it is Christmas Eve. She had gone away a madcap tomboy, Heathcliff's equal; she returns an elegant young lady, well-groomed and decked out in finery. During her absence Heathcliff has been neglected and when he appears, dirty and unkempt, he is so sensitive about the difference between them that he quickly dashes from the room. He sulks and goes without food until the next morning; then he asks Nelly to help tidy him up. She does this in time for him to be ready to meet the family and their visitors, the two young Lintons, as they return from church. An insolent remark from Edgar results in Heathcliff throwing a tureen of apple sauce over him and consequently being flogged and locked in his bedroom without any Christmas dinner. Catherine later contrives his escape but he is unable to eat the food Nelly offers him. He tells her he is thinking of his revenge on Hindley.

The chapter ends with a brief conversation between Nelly Dean and Lockwood in which he persuades her to continue with her story slowly, omitting nothing of consequence.

Commentary

For the first and only time in the novel we see something of the traditional life of the country as it could be seen in farm-houses such as Wuthering Heights – the great fires, the sumptuous Christmas fare of goose, cakes, tarts, fruit and mulled ale, the carol singers and the village band. It is shown to us to make our understanding of the desolation and spiritual violation more complete: Edgar and Isabella weep, Heathcliff is flogged, Catherine cannot eat her dinner and is 'in purgatory throughout the day'; even Nelly becomes melancholy at the memory of Christmases past, when old Mr Earnshaw was alive. The contrast with the simulated Christmas cheer is emphasised by Heathcliff's unchristian vow of revenge against Hindley; it begins a new phase of the action.

The fairy-tale element of the novel is reinforced by Nelly's metaphor of Heathcliff as 'a prince in disguise' but this happy picture soon turns sour as the ill-treated Heathcliff turns out after all to be an 'imp of Satan' (Chapter 4), opting to usurp God's function of punishing the wicked. Yet at no other point in the story do we feel such close sympathy with Heathcliff as in this chapter. He has overcome his feelings of misery and despair and has tried to 'be good', only to find himself an outcast. Later in the novel, when he is obsessed by bitterness and hate we should remember this moment of the withdrawal of love from him.

Chapter 8

Summary

In June 1778 Hareton Earnshaw is born but his birth marks a decline in the health of his mother, Frances, and later that year she dies in Hindley's arms. From that time Hindley behaves as if demented and life at the Heights falls into dissolution; the servants leave and the curate will no longer call. By the time Catherine is fifteen, in 1780, she has become a beauty and is courted by Edgar Linton. She seems to have less and less time for Heathcliff and he is hurt and miserable. One day when Hindley is absent, Edgar visits the Heights and, during a show of passion against Nelly, Catherine boxes his ears. The incident ends with the two becoming avowed lovers before Hindley's arrival drives Edgar swiftly homewards.

Commentary

Whilst this chapter forwards Edgar Linton's courtship of Catherine, it simultaneously maintains the reader's sympathy for Heathcliff by showing how he is constantly at a disadvantage; not only is his education completely neglected, but he is also compelled to labour at rough and dirty jobs around the farm for long hours with little recompense.

Chapter 9

Summary

Hindley arrives home drunk and threatens Nelly with the carving knife but she does not take his threats seriously. However, Hindley takes Hareton, carries him upstairs and holds him over the banister. At that moment Heathcliff enters downstairs and Hindley's attention is distracted so that he drops his son. By a reflex action, Heathcliff catches the child and sets him on his feet. Nelly, very angry, snatches the child away and goes into the kitchen with him, where Catherine enters: neither of them realise that Heathcliff has also come in and is on the other side of the room, hidden from sight. Catherine makes the confession to Nelly that she is going to marry Edgar Linton but that her real love is Heathcliff and had Hindley not degraded him she would never have agreed to marry Edgar. In the middle of this speech Nelly sees Heathcliff get up and steal out. After Catherine has added a few more confidences, Joseph enters and when they call Heathcliff to supper he does not respond. The night is one of violent storm and thunder but Catherine cannot settle. Searching for Heathcliff she gets drenched and then sits all night waiting for him to return. Next day she is taken ill with fever. She languishes for some while and as she gradually improves she is taken to Thrushcross Grange to convalesce; this results in old Mr and Mrs Linton both catching the fever and dying. Heathcliff does not return and three years later Catherine and Edgar are married.

Commentary

Though this chapter too covers the events of several years, most of it is taken up with the evening immediately following the final incident of the previous chapter. Heathcliff, overhears Catherine telling Nelly that she cannot marry him, Heathcliff, because he has been so degraded; already spiritually bruised by Catherine's increasing interest in Edgar, he does not hear her say how much she loves him. Catherine's great passionate statement of her love, culminating in the words, 'Nelly, I *am* Heathcliff' is one of the highlights of the novel; it shows Catherine deeply aware of the contrast between her love for Heathcliff and that for Edgar Linton. The weakness of her attachment to Edgar is made apparent by the change in narrative speed, for her marriage to him three years later, in 1783, is passed over in one brief paragraph.

Life at Wuthering Heights has now disintegrated entirely: Hindley is completely debauched, Heathcliff has disappeared mysteriously into the stormy night and Catherine goes to live with Edgar in Thrushcross Grange, taking Nelly with her; little Hareton is left to the drunken administration of his father.

Chapter 10

Summary

Following the breakdown of civilised life at Wuthering Heights, the story now moves to Thrushcross Grange. Chapter 10 begins in the present of the novel with Lockwood bemoaning a four weeks' sickness which he has endured since Nelly broke off her tale at the end of the previous chapter. Significantly placed between the account of Heathcliff's disappearance and that of his return, Lockwood's brief interpolation shows Heathcliff in yet another perspective: he has shown kindness to Lockwood both by sending him a brace of grouse and by making a sick visit and chatting amiably.

Commentary

After Heathcliff's visit, Nelly Dean is persuaded to continue her tale. For six months or so the married life of Catherine and Edgar seems to be happy and settled until, one evening in September 1783, Heathcliff reappears. Catherine is overjoyed to see him and, to Edgar's discomfort, makes much of him. Heathcliff establishes himself at Wuthering Heights with Hindley and, despite Nelly's feelings of disquiet, life at Thrushcross Grange proceeds smoothly; then Isabella discloses that she is in love with Heathcliff. In a moment of spite Catherine tells Heathcliff of her sister-in-law's passion and, though he brushes it aside, Nelly is convinced that he does not forget it.

Following our glimpse of Heathcliff's civility to Lockwood, Catherine's description of him to Isabella as 'an unreclaimed creature, without refinement, without cultivation ... a fierce, pitiless, wolfish man' brings us back to our original view with a shock of recognition. The contrast between his uncouth manners and the gentleness of Edgar is especially marked here.

Chapter 11

Summary
Nelly is often desperately worried about Hindley living at the Heights with his sworn enemy, so she decides to visit him. She meets Hareton at the gate and is dismayed to find him transformed into a violent, blaspheming little ruffian. Whilst she waits for Hindley to appear, Heathcliff comes to the door and Nelly turns away and makes for home. On Heathcliff's next visit to Thrushcross Grange Nelly sees him embrace Isabella in the garden and she draws Catherine's attention to this act. A quarrel results, first between Catherine and Heathcliff and then between Heathcliff and Edgar; during this latter trouble, Catherine locks the kitchen door with them all inside and throws the key into the fire. Goaded beyond endurance by Heathcliff, the gentle Edgar strikes out at him and then escapes through the back door. Catherine once more takes refuge in a fit of passion and rushes up to her own bedroom, locking herself in.

Commentary
The transformation of Hareton into an uncouth ragamuffin is not only part of Heathcliff's revenge on Hindley; it is also one of the many transformations that take place in the novel. This chapter contains, too, the first of several incidents in which various characters are locked into rooms. Keys and doors are significant symbols of domination. Here, Catherine tries, first, to impose her will on Heathcliff and Edgar and, secondly, to gain an advantage by locking herself away, believing that if she starves herself, her physical condition will cause Edgar anxiety.

Chapter 12

Summary
A bleak picture ensues; Catherine remains locked in her bedroom; Edgar stays in his study with his books; Isabella mopes in the garden; only Nelly goes stoically about her usual duties around Thrushcross Grange. When Catherine emerges from her room after three days, she is weak and feverish and suffering delirium. Her mind constantly reverts to life in Wuthering Heights and to her childhood with Heathcliff. Her ravings recall aspects of the story already significant to us: the clothes-press and the oak-

panelled bed of the room where Lockwood had his nightmare; the fir tree which tapped on the window; the death of old Mr Earnshaw and Hindley's ill-treatment of Heathcliff; the first visit to Thrushcross Grange.

When Edgar sees her he is shocked and blames Nelly who had made light of Catherine's condition. However, in her feverish state Catherine has realised the spiritual violation she committed on herself by marrying Edgar and rejects his love. Dr Kenneth, who had attended Catherine during her previous fever, is disturbed at her state but does what he can for her.

Commentary

In the midst of all this trouble it is discovered that Isabella has eloped with Heathcliff. Brontë makes little of the actual elopement, emphasising the plight of the little dog Fanny more than that of Isabella herself. By the end of this chapter it appears that all the characters are pursuing their own ends; we may recall Nelly's introduction of this phase of the story back in Chapter 10: 'Well, we *must* be for ourselves in the long run; the mild and generous are only more justly selfish than the domineering.'

Chapter 13

Summary

Catherine gradually recovers and Edgar at last carries her downstairs to the parlour. Close by, another room, the very room, in fact, which Lockwood now occupies, is fitted up as a bedroom so that Catherine does not fatigue herself by going up and downstairs; this is particularly important as we learn that Catherine is expecting a baby.

Two months after her marriage Isabella returns and is taken by Heathcliff to Wuthering Heights. She announces her arrival to Nelly in a letter which occupies most of the chapter. Isabella's picture of life at the Heights is a dreary one; filth and neglect have taken over; Hareton is dirty; Hindley unkempt and slovenly; none of the floors has been cleaned and the pewter dishes which Lockwood had observed on his first visit to the house are grey and dusty. Nicely brought up, Isabella is out of place here; her voice and manners grate on Joseph's senses and when she asks for her bedroom he takes her on a tour of the house, showing how unsuited every room is for her use. She finally drops to sleep in a chair beside the fire in the sitting-room and is there when Heathcliff enters.

Commentary

Here the narration is taken over by Isabella whose actual letter Nelly reads directly to Lockwood in the midst of her tale. The reader thus sees the household at Wuthering Heights and the house itself in yet another perspective. We should observe Isabella's comments about the eyes of both Hareton and Hindley, for the 'look of Catherine' she sees in them is recalled on several occasions later in the novel; in Chapter 33, for instance, Heathcliff is disconcerted to find the eyes of Hareton and the second Catherine reflecting the eyes of his own beloved Catherine.

Chapter 14

Summary
Nelly tells Edgar of Isabella's return and begs forgiveness for her but he refuses this plea on the grounds that he has nothing to forgive. He refuses to write to her and insists that there shall be no communication between the two houses; nevertheless, he allows Nelly to go to Wuthering Heights that afternoon. When she arrives there she finds the house dismal and neglected and Isabella looking like a slattern; Heathcliff, on the other hand, looks quite gentlemanly. Nelly tells him of Catherine's illness and he demands to see her; he insists that, to avoid trouble, Nelly shall help him to this end and she reluctantly agrees to take a letter to her mistress. At this point in the tale Dr Kenneth arrives to see Lockwood and we are brought back again into the present.

Commentary
Brontë here underlines the contrast between Edgar's coldness and Heathcliff's passionate intensity. Heathcliff does nothing by halves, loving and hating with the whole of his being; he shows an entirely self-ish hatred of Isabella and an entirely selfless love for Catherine, fuelled by a burning passion within him. Edgar, on the other hand, withholds even his anger from Isabella and merely expresses his sorrow at her loss; further, Nelly depicts him tending Catherine through 'duty' and 'humanity', not through love.

Chapter 15

Summary
Four days after Nelly's visit to Wuthering Heights, on a Sunday when the household are at church, she gives Heathcliff's letter to Catherine. Before Catherine has had time fully to understand its import, Heathcliff enters the room and clasps her in his arms. On seeing her wasted state he is distraught and tears and words of agony are wrung from him. Catherine feels she is soon to die and her greatest anguish is the loss of Heathcliff but she has no pity for him, only blame; the pair are in torment and their future appears to promise nothing but torment. When Edgar is seen returning from church Heathcliff tries to leave but Catherine clings to him and he stays. By the time Edgar comes into the room Catherine has fainted away and Heathcliff places her in Edgar's arms and walks from the room.

Commentary

The calmness of Catherine's sick state is violently broken in upon by Heathcliff's entry. The show of passion which ensues is of animal intensity: Heathcliff grinds his teeth, gnashes, foams 'like a mad dog'. In this, their last encounter, they rend each other's souls. The spiritual destruction they wreak upon each other is apparent in Heathcliff's declaration that 'misery, and degradation, and death, and nothing that God or Satan could inflict would have parted us' had Catherine not done it herself, which both echoes and negates St Paul's assertion of the redemptive power of the love of God: 'neither death, nor life, nor angels, nor principalities, nor powers, nor things present, nor things to come, nor height, nor depth, nor any other creature, shall be able to separate us from the love of God' (Romans 8: 38 – 9). From the words they exchange now comes Heathcliff's conviction that Catherine continually haunts him; the 'twenty years hence' of her prophecy is uncannily recalled not to Heathcliff but to Lockwood in his nightmare.

Chapter 16

Summary

In this short chapter the second Cathy is born and the first dies, without fully regaining consciousness. Nelly expresses a somewhat conventional philosophy about death, suggesting that Catherine has gone to 'perfect peace', 'divine rest', but it is to convince herself, for she does not really believe that Catherine can be 'happy in the other world'. When she goes into the garden to tell Heathcliff of the night's events he knows already that Catherine is dead. Nelly is inwardly distressed at his agony and realises that, despite his wildness, he shares a common humanity. Her pious remarks about Catherine, however, rouse Heathcliff to fury and he cries out to Catherine to haunt him for ever; his animal qualities take over and Nelly leaves him because she knows that she cannot help him.

Catherine's funeral does not take place until the Friday after her death; from compassion for Heathcliff Nelly opens the window of the death-chamber on Tuesday evening whilst Edgar is resting and Heathcliff enters to take a final goodbye. During his visit he opens the locket around Catherine's neck, throws out Edgar's lock of hair and places his own inside. Nelly sees what has happened and twines the two together inside the locket. Catherine is buried in a corner of the churchyard, away from the tombs of both the Lintons and the Earnshaws in a spot where the wildness of heath and moor have encroached.

Commentary

Heathcliff now appears to be a creature beyond redemption. With Catherine dead he believes that he has lost his soul (we should remember her words in Chapter 9, 'Nelly, I *am* Heathcliff'); his only hope lies in the possibility of her ghost remaining with him.

Chapter 17

Summary

The first main phase of the story is now ending and the second phase is about to begin. The bright, cheerful weather of the preceding three weeks breaks on the evening of the funeral and storm, wind and snow set in, bringing turbulence and unrest instead of the hoped-for calm. Suddenly, whilst Nelly sits nursing the infant Cathy, Isabella rushes in, scantily clad, dripping wet and full of excitement; she has escaped from Wuthering Heights and Heathcliff. She changes into fresh clothes and, over a cup of tea, tells Nelly what has happened.

Hindley, intending to go to Catherine's funeral, has remained sober overnight but when he rises in the morning he begins to drink heavily and is thus unfit to go to the church. He and Isabella stay in the house all day. When Heathcliff returns at midnight Hindley decides to keep him locked out for five minutes and kill him as he tries to get in. Isabella, however, despite her wish to be rid of Heathcliff, cannot countenance his murder. She warns him what is about to happen and as he breaks through the window Hindley tries unsuccessfully to kill him and is himself injured. Heathcliff then proceeds to kick and beat his unconscious adversary until Isabella at last manages to summon Joseph.

Next morning Hindley looks very weak and sick and as Isabella talks to him she deliberately goads Heathcliff until he throws a knife at her. She flees from the room and escapes from the house.

Once her tale is told, Isabella leaves Thrushcross Grange in case Heathcliff tries to take her back and she makes her way to London where, a few months later, Linton is born. Heathcliff takes no immediate steps to claim his son but vows to take him when he wants him. Fortunately, Nelly explains, this time does not arrive until Linton is twelve years old and after Isabella's death. Six months after the death of Catherine, Hindley too dies, following a night of drinking. It now transpires that Wuthering Heights and all the Earnshaw property is mortgaged to Heathcliff and Hareton is left destitute.

Commentary

Isabella's interpolated story fills in further details of life at the Heights and makes clear the bitter hatred which exists between Hindley and Heathcliff. Observe the kind of imagery she uses to describe Heathcliff: 'sharp cannibal teeth', 'basilisk eyes', 'clouded windows of hell' (his eyes again), 'fiend';

the overpowering picture is of one not entirely human and when Nelly claims, 'He's a human being', Isabella denies it.

As far as chapters are concerned we are now exactly half way through the novel; the story of the first generation is now over and the births of Cathy and Linton herald the opening of the story of the second generation.

Chapter 18

Summary
Nelly passes swiftly over the next twelve years, merely establishing the charm of Cathy's character and describing her sheltered life. When, in 1797, Isabella realises that she is dying, she begs Edgar to visit her and to take Linton home with him. So Edgar leaves Cathy in Nelly's care and goes to visit his sister. Whilst he is away Cathy, who had always longed to visit Penistone Crags, tricks Nelly and makes her way there, some five and a half miles, on her pony and accompanied by several dogs. Nelly, unaware of the deceit, does not go to search for her until the evening; when she reaches Wuthering Heights, which is between Thrushcross Grange and the Crags, she sees one of the dogs outside and realises that Cathy is there. Cathy has met Hareton and the housekeeper at the Heights but both Heathcliff and Joseph are away for the day. Hareton had gone with her to Penistone Crags and the two of them are on the best of terms. Nelly is angry, however, and Cathy becomes defiant; an argument ensues, during which Cathy learns that Hareton is her cousin and Hareton and the housekeeper learn that Edgar has gone to fetch Linton. As they return to Thrushcross Grange, Nelly explains that Edgar would be distressed to learn that Cathy had visited the Heights and might even dismiss Nelly for negligence. Cathy agrees, therefore, to say nothing of the visit.

Commentary
This is our first view of the adult Hareton and, despite his surliness, our opinion is, on the whole, favourable. Later, when affection grows between him and Cathy we should remember this, their first encounter. There is again emphasis on the Earnshaw eyes which both Cathy and Hareton possess; this prepares us for Heathcliff's agitation in Chapter 33 when the two turn upon him the eyes of the dead Catherine.

Chapter 19

Summary
Edgar writes home to announce Isabella's death and to ask Nelly to prepare a room for Linton, whom he is bringing back with him. Cathy is impatient for their arrival and is delighted to see her father again. She is

introduced to Linton who is frail and fretful; her kindness, however, cheers him up and they get him off to bed.

Suddenly Joseph arrives at the Grange and insists that he must take Linton back to Wuthering Heights. Edgar realises that he will be unable to keep the boy but he will not wake him up and send him away that night, so Joseph returns without him.

Commentary

Linton's arrival at the Grange may be compared with Heathcliff's first arrival at Wuthering Heights. Physically a striking contrast to his father, he is nevertheless a disruptive element. Unlike Cathy, he appears to have inherited the worst traits of both his parents. Nelly's lack of sympathy in the telling – 'A pale, delicate, effeminate boy. . .a sickly peevishness in his aspect', prepares the reader for what is to follow. Joseph, 'donned in his Sunday garments' is an ill omen and though he returns empty-handed we know that trouble is to come.

Chapter 20

Summary

Edgar sends Nelly next morning to deliver Linton to Heathcliff. When he is awoken at five o'clock, Linton refuses to get up and go with her, so Edgar has to help get him off. Isabella had never told her son about his father and the boy can hardly believe he has one; though Nelly tries to convince him that his father will love him she does not really believe this herself. With Linton on Cathy's pony, he and Nelly journey to Wuthering Heights. Heathcliff is shocked at Linton's sickly appearance, but claims ownership of him – 'he's *mine*' – for his son represents his possibility of triumph over and revenge upon both the Lintons and the Earnshaws. Nelly returns to Thrushcross Grange ill at ease.

Commentary

Our fears for Linton are only partly allayed by Heathcliff's determination to rear him as a gentleman. We should notice that, although the boy is only twelve years old, Heathcliff talks of not wishing him to die, 'till I [am] certain of being his successor'.

Chapter 21

Summary

After her initial distress at Linton's departure, Cathy calms down. Two years pass, during which Nelly gets occasional news of life at Wuthering Heights from the housekeeper. The accounts of Linton are very uncomplimentary. The housekeeper leaves and Zillah, whom Lockwood had met on his visit to the Heights, takes her place.

Cathy's birthday, being also the anniversary of her mother's death, is not a time when Edgar indulges in celebrations. The day she is sixteen – we now learn that her birthday is March 20th – she is given permission to go with Nelly to look at a colony of grouse up on the moor. They set out and Cathy leads her further and further from home until, when they are about a mile distant from Wuthering Heights they come upon Heathcliff and Hareton. Despite Nelly's objections, Cathy accepts an invitation to go to Wuthering Heights and there she sees Linton again, now a tall youth of fifteen. She realises then that Heathcliff is her uncle and he tells her that the two families have kept separate from each other because he and Edgar had a quarrel in the past.

Heathcliff confides to Nelly his plan of marrying Cathy and Linton to each other, pretending that this is in order to give Cathy security. Linton, however, seems intent on thwarting this plan, refusing at first to accompany Cathy out into the garden. Hareton is sent out with her and Heathcliff proceeds to tell Nelly how much he rejoices in Hareton's brutishness. Yet he compares him very favourably with his own son; 'gold put to the use of paving-stones', whilst Linton is 'tin polished to ape a service of silver'. Linton is finally persuaded to follow Hareton and Cathy outside. He arrives there at the moment when Cathy is asking Hareton about the inscription over the door; it is the very inscription which Lockwood had drawn attention to on his first visit to Wuthering Heights; ironically, it is Hareton's own name: 'Hareton Earnshaw' and the date 1500; Hareton cannot read, however, and Cathy and Linton spitefully mock his ignorance.

Nelly and Cathy return home in the afternoon and next day Cathy tells her father about her visit. Greatly distressed, he tries to show her Heathcliff's character but, having been brought up in such gentle and loving circumstances, she finds it difficult to comprehend. He requests her not to associate with the family at the Heights. As the weeks pass Cathy becomes very secretive and one day Nelly discovers a cache of love letters from Linton in a drawer where Cathy had previously kept her childhood treasures. It turns out that a small milk-boy has been acting as go-between. Nelly, though very angry at the deceit, is persuaded by Cathy not to tell Edgar. She agrees to burn the letters and this is done. Nelly then answers the last letter by a stiff note, sent with the milk-boy, asking Linton to refrain from sending further notes.

Commentary

This long chapter considerably advances the plot. The pattern of Heathcliff's revenge now begins to take shape: Hareton suffers brutish degradation to atone for the indignities his father heaped on Heathcliff's head. Linton and Cathy are to be married to each other, in order to secure Thrushcross Grange as well as Wuthering Heights to Heathcliff.

Chapter 22

Summary
Summer and autumn pass and towards the end of harvest-time Edgar catches a severe cold which affects his lungs. Whilst he is confined indoors Nelly has to replace him as Cathy's companion on her walks. One day when, despite the threat of rain, Cathy refuses to forgo her walk, they go into the park and Nelly notices that Cathy is constantly on the verge of tears because she is worried about her father. Nelly tries to cheer her up and as Cathy climbs on the wall to gather some rosehips her hat falls on the other side; she jumps down to get it but cannot climb back up again. The nearby gate in the wall is locked; Nelly is just about to run back and get the key when Heathcliff approaches on his horse and stops to speak to Cathy. He tells her that Linton is dying for love of her; Nelly maintains that he is talking nonsense and breaks the lock to let Cathy inside. Heathcliff, declaring that he will be away from home for a week, begs Cathy to visit Linton; he then rides away. Cathy is so worried about Linton that Nelly agrees to accompany her to Wuthering Heights the next day.

Commentary
Again a locked door leads to a crisis; Cathy, locked out of the gardens of the Grange is at Heathcliff's mercy, though at this time he does nothing more than talk. Yet it is this incident which leads to her later imprisonment in the Heights. We should observe how Nelly is repeatedly led into betraying Edgar's trust in her. In the belief that she was acting for the best she had again and again helped the older Catherine and Heathcliff to deceive Edgar; now she does the same for Cathy, constantly protecting her master from knowledge which he ought to possess.

Chapter 23

Summary
Next day, after a wet night, Nelly accompanies Cathy to Wuthering Heights. When they enter the kitchen they find Joseph sitting smoking and drinking ale beside a roaring fire. Heathcliff is absent but a voice from the inner room indicates that Linton is there. During his father's absence the servants are studiously neglecting him; his fire is nearly out and he is coughing and feverish. He is in querulous mood and complaining about everything. Nelly makes up the fire but gets no thanks. Cathy and Linton soon begin to quarrel over the relationship between their parents and Cathy gets so angry that she pushes his chair violently; he immediately falls into a paroxysm of coughing which frightens both Cathy and Nelly, though the latter is not altogether sympathetic as she suspects that

he is exaggerating his condition. Linton tries to persuade them to prolong their visit but Nelly insists that they return to Thrushcross Grange.

On their way back Cathy and Nelly, in their turn, argue and Nelly forbids Cathy to return to Wuthering Heights the next day. Whilst trudging between the two houses, Nelly's shoes and stockings have been soaked through and this brings on a chill which confines her to her bed for the next three weeks. Cathy is a very attentive nurse and Nelly never suspects that after six in the evening, when her duties with Edgar and Nelly are finished, her young mistress rides over the moor to visit Linton at Wuthering Heights.

Commentary

We have observed Cathy's selfishness in the last chapter. Here she thinks nothing of forcing Nelly to walk across the damp moor whilst she rides her pony. We also see yet another example of her deceit as she once more betrays her father's and Nelly's trust by going secretively to Wuthering Heights. The imagery of keys and locked doors is used by Cathy to attempt to assert her independence; 'The grange is not a prison . . . you are not my jailer' she tells Nelly, reminding her at the same time that she, Cathy can climb over the wall, just as she did the previous day when Heathcliff accosted her.

There is a striking contrast between the passion that Catherine and Heathcliff evinced for each other and the emasculated emotion of protective pity that Cathy believes is love for her weakling cousin.

Chapter 24

Summary

After three weeks of being confined to her room, Nelly is much improved and the first evening she is able to sit up she asks Cathy to read to her. Cathy does so with a bad grace and much impatience. She behaves in the same way the following evening and on the third evening she complains of a headache and goes to her bedroom.

When Nelly goes to her room to see how she is she discovers that Cathy is not there, so she sits by the window to await the truant's return. On her return, Cathy at first lies about what she has been doing but then confesses that she has regularly been visiting Linton at Wuthering Heights in the evenings: she now takes up the narration and describes her visits, dwelling on Linton's difficult temper and mocking Hareton's attempts to learn to read; she ends by begging Nelly not to tell Edgar of her escapades. Nelly, however, has deceived her master too often and this time she tells him the whole story. He forbids Cathy to visit Wuthering Heights again but he agrees to write to Linton and give him permission to come to Thrushcross Grange.

Commentary

Again the shift in narrative stance gives the reader a view of events from a different standpoint. Despite Cathy's attitude towards Linton and Hareton respectively, we recognise that the former is utterly selfish and self-centred and we see in the latter some positive signs of grace, though he is, as yet, unrefined and boorish.

Chapter 25

Summary

This short chapter does not much advance the plot but it moves us forward in time some half a year. During this period Cathy and Linton remain separated, though Edgar and Linton conduct a correspondence; it is restrained on Edgar's part but Linton, coached by Heathcliff, constantly begs to be allowed to meet his cousin. Edgar's health is steadily deteriorating and he becomes increasingly concerned about Cathy's future; he believes that her only hope of security lies in marriage with Linton. At last, therefore, he reluctantly agrees to allow the two to meet on the moors once a week to walk or ride together under Nelly's surveillance. No one at Thrushcross Grange knows how sick Linton really is.

Commentary

The opening words of this chapter make us realise that the story is coming to an end; Nelly is now recounting events that happened less than a year previously. The immediacy of the tale is emphasised as she addresses Lockwood in the present. We are reminded, too, that he is a stranger and has no part in the life of the Earnshaws and the Lintons; we understand that their play must be played out without his intervention.

Chapter 26

Summary

After Edgar has given his permission, Cathy and Nelly set out one day in late summer to meet Linton. Their meeting-place is to be the guide-stone at the crossroads which, we were told in Chapter 11, Nelly and Hindley had once held a favourite spot. When they arrive there, however, a little herd-boy awaits them with a message from Linton asking them to meet him closer to Wuthering Heights. With some misgivings on Nelly's part they go forward and they are within a quarter of a mile of Wuthering Heights before they come upon Linton lying out on the heath waiting for them. They are shocked to see how pale and feeble he is but he tries to assure them that he is well. He is clearly not really pleased to see them, though he is terrified at the possibility that they will go away early. Whilst they are talking he drops to sleep and awakes with a start, fearful of Heathcliff's approach. Cathy promises to return the following Thursday and she and Nelly leave.

Commentary
Here, as so often in the novel, the weather matches the movement of the plot. The sultry, threatening day prepares us for the menace which seems to hang over Linton. The physical violence which we have witnessed earlier is replaced by an unspecified violence, more frightening in that our imaginations run wild as we try to envisage Heathcliff's methods of dominating his sickly son.

Chapter 27

Summary
During the week which follows, Edgar's condition deteriorates swiftly. By the time Thursday arrives Cathy has little wish to leave him in order to visit her cousin but she agrees to go for a short while during the afternoon.

Linton is no better but he is obsessed by fear for his own life and despair that he is betraying Cathy. At the same time, his abject terror of Heathcliff prevents him from disclosing the plot which he has been compelled to participate in. Whilst they speak together Heathcliff suddenly arrives. He greets Nelly and asks after Edgar, not because he is concerned about Edgar's health but because he fears Linton may die first. Cathy and Nelly are tricked into helping Linton back to Wuthering Heights and when they go inside Heathcliff turns the key in the lock: they are prisoners. Cathy, in a fierce display of spirits which reminds us of her mother, tries to regain the key from Heathcliff; she bites at his hand as it clutches the key and he retaliates by beating her violently about the head.

When Heathcliff goes out to look to the horses, Linton, relieved but fretful, confesses that he has helped in the plot in order to force Cathy to marry him the next morning. Cathy's concern is now for her father who will miss her; she immediately agrees to marry Linton but Heathcliff insists that they are to wait until the morning. He locks them in the housekeeper's room and next day takes Cathy away; Nelly, however, is kept prisoner for another four days and nights, with Hareton acting as her jailer.

Commentary
A key is once more at the centre of the action; this time the locked door represents imprisonment for Cathy and Nelly and their domination by Heathcliff. We should notice that Heathcliff finally imprisons them, not in Catherine's old room, but in Zillah's room where, we are told, the window is too narrow to escape. Throughout the novel there is a meticulous

attention to detail which helps to realise the whole setting for us. When Cathy tells Heathcliff that she will not take her eyes from his face we should remember the emphasis made earlier on the fact that Cathy has the Earnshaw eyes, for she looks at him with the eyes of her mother. Several chapters further on (Chapter 33) Heathcliff is disturbed and disarmed when Hareton and Cathy, both of whom have the Earnshaw eyes, look up at him at the same moment.

Chapter 28

Summary

Nelly is released from her imprisonment by Zillah, who tells her that the whole village thinks she has been drowned in the marsh. During the time that Nelly has been shut up in Wuthering Heights the marriage between Linton and Cathy has taken place. She learns from Linton that, although Edgar is very ill, Cathy has not been allowed to return to him; Linton, now her husband, is also her jailer and, apart from Heathcliff, he alone knows where the key to her apartment is hidden.

When Nelly realises that she is unable to free Cathy she returns to Thrushcross Grange where she finds her master very close to death. She sends some men to Wuthering Heights to rescue Cathy but they come back without her. However, in the night Cathy arrives home, having escaped through the window of her mother's old bedroom, the very window beside which, a few months later, Lockwood experiences his nightmare. Our attention is drawn to the fact that there is a fir tree close to the window, down which Cathy climbs; it is this fir tree which knocks against the window when Lockwood sleeps in the room. We should notice that at this time, September 1801, the window can be opened, whereas when Lockwood is there he observes that 'the hook [is] soldered into the staple' (Chapter 3). Cathy's escape from Wuthering Heights is the last of a series of escapes which began with that of Catherine and Heathcliff from Hindley's tyranny on the Sunday late in 1777 when they first ventured to look in the window at Thrushcross Grange.

Commentary

Cathy arrives in time to see her father die. Of his generation only Heathcliff and Nelly herself remain. The three members of the younger generation bear a strange heritage: Cathy, the only child of the union between the households of Linton and Earnshaw, is dispossessed of the Linton lands and wealth; Hareton, the direct descendant of the Earnshaw family, is dispossessed of Wuthering Heights; Linton Heathcliff, the child of hate produced through the union of Heathcliff with the Linton family and now married to Cathy, owns the whole of the Linton and Earnshaw inheritance.

Chapter 29

Summary

Heathcliff waits until after Edgar's funeral before he comes to Thrushcross Grange to take possession and to bear Cathy back to Wuthering Heights. It is the last phase of the story. The first Catherine had married and moved from Wuthering Heights to Thrushcross Grange; now the second Cathy, married to Linton, is to move from Thrushcross Grange to Wuthering Heights. Whilst she is collecting her things together, Heathcliff talks to Nelly, the one person he has known throughout his life. The portrait of Catherine Earnshaw, which hangs, together with that of Edgar Linton, on the wall of the library where they are sitting, appears to loosen Heathcliff's tongue.

He tells Nelly that the previous day, whilst Edgar's grave was being dug beside that of his wife, he had opened Catherine's coffin and looked upon her face; he had then bribed the sexton to pull out the side of his (Heathcliff's) coffin when he is finally buried next to Catherine and to slide the side from hers too, so that they might be together in death. This story brings back to his mind the evening of Catherine's funeral when he had also attempted to open her coffin, only to become convinced that she was not in the grave but with him on earth. Catherine was so real to him that he talked to her as he returned to Wuthering Heights. When he arrived there, however, he found that Hindley and Isabella had locked him out. Heathcliff's narration gives us a startling new perspective on the events recounted by Isabella in Chapter 17. Catherine's presence, just beyond the threshold of reality, called to him from the Heights and he was denied the comfort of entering and being with her again.

Commentary

The time shift and double narration of this incident serve the purpose of recalling to the reader's mind Heathcliff's torment at Catherine's death and his agonised plea for her to haunt him (Chapter 16). His passionate and moving words to Nelly revive our reluctant sympathy for him at a moment when we might well feel the deepest repugnanace. The chapter ends with Heathcliff taking Cathy away to Wuthering Heights and asking Nelly to send Catherine's portrait to him the next day.

Chapter 30

Summary

The story is now taken up by Zillah, the housekeeper at Wuthering Heights. She meets Nelly on the moor one day and tells her of the happenings at the Heights. Cathy is given no help in nursing Linton and soon after her arrival he dies. She herself is ill and stays in her room for a fortnight.

When she comes down, Hareton tries to befriend her but he is repulsed and gives up his attempts. Zillah's efforts to make Hareton presentable for Cathy parallel events in Chapter 7 when Nelly helps Heathcliff to tidy himself up for the Christmas party at the Heights just after Catherine's return from Thrushcross Grange.

Commentary

Nelly feels anxious and concerned about Cathy's situation but she does not know what she can do to relieve it. This is the end of her story, her conversation with Zillah having taken place about six weeks earlier, just before Lockwood arrived at the Grange. He takes over the narration in the last paragraph of the chapter and explains to the reader that he now feels well enough to leave Thrushcross Grange and go to London for the next six months.

Chapter 31

Summary

We have now moved in Nelly Dean's memory from 1771 to the present of the novel, 1802. Lockwood, who through his diary is the principal narrator of the story, has been auditor of Nelly's tale since his adventures at Wuthering Heights related in the first three chapters; now he takes up the narration again.

The day after Nelly had finished her story he goes to Wuthering Heights; he bears with him a note from Nelly to Cathy. This he gives to her surreptitiously but, clearly believing it is a note from Lockwood himself, she throws it off her lap and remarks upon it. On Lockwood telling her it is a note from Nelly, Cathy tries to take it up again but it is snatched away by Hareton. However, Hareton is moved by Cathy's tears and returns it rather ungraciously. Similarly, after a conversation about books in which Cathy mocks at him, Hareton brings a bundle of books from his room and throws them in her lap. She, however, continues to scorn him and finally, in a fit of rage, he hurls them into the fire. Lockwood, who is the audience for all this, engages our sympathy for Hareton by his understanding tone.

Now Heathcliff enters and Lockwood is welcomed and invited to dinner. He leaves Wuthering Heights with the somewhat vain thought that had he and Cathy fallen in love it would have turned into a fairy-tale romance.

Commentary

Here, again, Heathcliff is seen to be haunted by Catherine, this time seeing her face in Hareton's as the young man, discontented and unhappy, pushes his way out of the house.

Chapter 32

Summary
The story is taken up eight months later in September 1802 when Lockwood, visiting a friend in the north, finds himself close to Gimmerton and decides to stay the night at Thrushcross Grange. When he arrives there, however, he learns that Nelly is now at Wuthering Heights. As nothing is ready for him at the Grange he leaves the new housekeeper to make the necessary preparations whilst he walks over to the Heights.

There, he has the impression that things are much improved: the gate opens to his touch and the garden yields a fragrance of flowers among the fruit trees; it is a warm day and all the doors and windows are open, though there is a fine coal fire burning in the hearth. As he approaches the house, Lockwood hears Cathy and Hareton conversing together; Hareton is receiving a reading lesson. The lesson concludes and the two leave the house; Lockwood makes his way round to the kitchen where he finds Nelly sewing and singing whilst Joseph moans and complains. Nelly recognises Lockwood immediately and invites him in. He very quickly learns that Heathcliff died three months previously and Nelly launches into the sequel of her story.

A fortnight after Lockwood's departure for London, Heathcliff asks Nelly to go to Wuthering Heights. She is pleased to be there with Cathy, though she finds life at the Heights depressing; Cathy is restless and miserable, Hareton morose and Heathcliff shuns all society. After a while, however, Nelly notices that Cathy is trying to be friends with Hareton and this, to the disgust of Joseph, she finally achieves. By the time Lockwood arrives Nelly is confident that their wedding will soon take place.

Commentary
The whole atmosphere of this chapter is lighter. Lockwood, as usual, is an observant narrator and draws our attention to salient points – doors and windows at Wuthering Heights are no longer locked and there is an air of loving companionship within the house.

Chapter 33

Summary
The friendship between Cathy and Hareton develops swiftly. Nelly is horrified to find Hareton uprooting some of Joseph's blackcurrant trees in order to plant flowers, for she knows that this will cause trouble. Whilst they are all having breakfast Cathy silently teases Hareton, until a smothered laugh from him draws Heathcliff's angry attention to them. A moment later Joseph enters, complaining about the blackcurrant trees;

this results in a violent exchange between Cathy and Heathcliff in which she accuses him of stealing both her and Hareton's lands and money and he attacks her furiously, seizing her by the hair. Hareton attempts to intervene but intervention proves unnecessary, for Heathcliff's passion subsides as swiftly as it arose; he looks intently into Cathy's face and then pushes her from him, warning her to keep out of his way.

That afternoon, whilst Heathcliff is out, Cathy and Hareton sit talking together and she begins to speak of Heathcliff's conduct towards Hindley; Hareton, however, will hear no ill of Heathcliff. When the latter comes in, the two young people look up at him, both with the eyes of Catherine Earnshaw. He is very disturbed and sends Cathy out of the room; Hareton follows; when Nelly is about to do the same Heathcliff requests her to stay. In a strangely moving monologue he tells Nelly that now he has the representatives of Earnshaws and Lintons in his power he has lost the desire for revenge. He feels that Cathy and Hareton are the only substantial things in his life; he has difficulty remembering to eat and drink, or even to breathe, or keep his heart beating. Hareton, especially, agitates him; not only is the younger man startlingly like Catherine Earnshaw but he also seems a personification of Heathcliff's own youth to the extent that he appears to have no independent life as a human being.

Commentary

In Heathcliff's speech we become aware both of the stifled aspirations of his childhood and also of the suppressed torment of his adult life. His whole yearning is towards the time when he will be with Catherine again though he feels that, with his robust constitution, he can hardly hope for an early death. The poetic power of Brontë's language transforms Heathcliff for us again into a man to be pitied, if not to be understood.

Chapter 34

Summary

Heathcliff now avoids all company. He does not join the others at meals and when Nelly serves him with food he seems unable to eat. His behaviour becomes so odd that it makes Nelly nervous, yet his whole demeanour is changed and he appears to be excited and joyful. For several days he neither eats nor sleeps, despite Nelly's anxiety; on the third day she tries to persuade him to send for a minister to talk to him; on the fourth day she sends Hareton for Dr Kenneth but Heathcliff locks his door and refuses to see the doctor.

Then the bright April weather changes. After a night of pouring rain Nelly finds Heathcliff dead beside the open window of the room that had once been Catherine's. The rain has beaten in upon him and the bed-clothes are soaking; his hair and face are wet. Nelly hasps the window which, we should remember, Heathcliff himself had wrenched open in Chapter 3: Heathcliff now joins Catherine and Edgar in a corner of the churchyard.

So the story ends, yet we are left wondering whether it is an end or a beginning. The country folk around believe that Heathcliff still walks the moors; Joseph affirms that he has seen both Catherine and Heathcliff on every rainy night since Heathcliff's death; a little shepherd boy asserts that he has seen them in the shelter of the hill. As for Cathy and Hareton, they are to be married on New Year's Day, 1803 and will go, together with Nelly, to live at Thrushcross Grange. Wuthering Heights will be left in the care of Joseph who will live in the kitchen quarters. As Lockwood leaves, deliberately avoiding a meeting with the young couple, the novel has come full circle; it began with Lockwood's first visit to Heathcliff at Wuthering Heights; it ends with his last visit to Wuthering Heights and the graves of Heathcliff, Catherine and Edgar.

Commentary

This last chapter picks up many of the themes which occur earlier in the book – the references to eyes and teeth, the emphasis on heaven and hell, the idea of Heathcliff as a goblin, but the roaring fire of the Heights is noticeably absent; it dies, it needs rekindling; the coals have to be blown red. Heathcliff's death at the window of Catherine's room vividly recalls that earlier scene of Lockwood's nightmare, beside that same window (Chapter 3); then Lockwood described the blood from the little ghost's wrists soaking the bed-clothes. Now, although Heathcliff's hand is grazed, no blood flows; the bed-clothes, however, are soaked with the rain; and now the window flaps open, no longer a separator, for Heathcliff is free to go to Catherine at last.

3 THEMES AND ISSUES

3.1 THE PLOT

When *Wuthering Heights* was first published in 1847 many readers found it confused, difficult and obscure. It is not surprising! An improbable plot set in a remote landscape and enacted by passionate and violent characters, it was unlike any novel they knew and indeed we may still see it as a unique creation. Yet, at the same time, it is exciting, powerful and, despite the unconventionality of its principal protagonists, infused with a strong sense of realism.

The enclosed world of the novel centres on two houses and two families. There has been an Earnshaw at Wuthering Heights since 1500 and Lintons at Thrushcross Grange probably as long. There appears to have been little intercourse between the two families and scarcely any with the outside world. At the time of the action of the novel the nearby village of Gimmerton has few dealings with the two houses; it supplies the servants and the curate teaches the children; Dr Kenneth ministers to the families in times of sickness and Mr Green the lawyer overlooks their legal affairs; but we never hear of the young people of either family going to the village, except to the kirk on Sundays, or indeed associating with companions from any other houses in the vicinity. Nelly talks of meeting people in Gimmerton and several of the adults make trips to other places. Early in the story Mr Earnshaw goes to Liverpool and brings Heathcliff back home with him; Hindley is sent to college and brings back a wife; Heathcliff runs away and comes back transformed into a gentleman; Isabella escapes from Wuthering Heights and goes to London. However, when they depart, Nelly, who knows so much of the families' histories, passes silently over the time of their absence as though their lives cease whilst they are away. Even Mr Lockwood possesses reality for us only when he is in the neighbourhood of the Grange and his first stay there is some thirty years after the chronological beginning of our story.

Into this rather insular community Heathcliff is thrust, an alien figure, 'a dirty, ragged, black-haired child', a 'gipsy brat' (Chapter 4). Picked up by old Mr Earnshaw off the streets of Liverpool, Heathcliff's origins remain a mystery but his effect on the family is instantaneously disruptive. Though he is washed and dressed in clean clothes, the children reject him and he is left to sleep on the landing. This neglect results in Nelly who should have looked after him being temporarily banished from the house: when she returns a few days later she observes that Catherine and Heathcliff are already 'very thick'. It is probably the first time in his short life that Heathcliff has experienced affection and he repays it with a profound love and undying devotion. Yet, though he engenders love in Catherine, he arouses hate in Hindley and the rift that now develops in the family is never healed: father is set against son, brother against sister. When Hindley is sent away to college it is less to educate him than to get him out of the house; meanwhile, Heathcliff is treated like a privileged, even a pampered son. At Mr Earnshaw's death, however, the positions are reversed: Hindley returns as head of the household and the favoured child is systematically brutalised by neglect and ill-treatment. Whatever Hindley has learnt at college it is not tolerance and, though Heathcliff is no more than thirteen years old, Hindley wreaks a bitter revenge on him; the boy is relegated to the position of servant, deprived of education and sent to work on the farm.

Love, however, is able to triumph over physical ills; whilst he retains Catherine's affection Heathcliff is inviolable; it is not his degradation but Catherine's vision of elegance that leads to catastrophe. The attractions of graceful clothes and gracious living which Catherine encounters when she is taken into Thrushcross Grange subtly take control of her. Heathcliff is left outside in the cold in more ways than one. When they are both outside the window, dirty and neglected, they are, nevertheless, happy; inside the window, in the beautiful drawing-room of Thrushcross Grange, Edgar and Isabella are quarrelling and unhappy with each other. The moment that Catherine passes from one side to the other of that window there is an end of all happiness for her and Heathcliff. Until this time they have both been children of nature responding to every situation simply and directly; now Catherine is enticed by 'fine clothes and flattery' (Chapter 7). When she returns to Wuthering Heights her natural impulses are inhibited and she has become fastidious: she hardly dares to touch the dogs in case they soil her new clothes; Nelly can be kissed gently but not hugged; only the sight of Heathcliff makes Catherine forget her own splendour in her rush to embrace and kiss him; but the momentary lapse in social dignity is immediately followed by criticism: 'If you wash your face, and brush your hair it will be all right. But you are so dirty!' Heathcliff has become an outsider again. He has borne remarkably well his banishment by Hindley and his exclusion from Thrushcross Grange but the deprivation of love implied in Catherine's rebuke is spiritually appalling. In the anguish of his (still childish) soul he cries out against society's demands, 'I shall be as dirty as I please, and I like to be dirty, and I will be dirty'. Nothing in the novel equals the desolation of the child's soul over that Christmas holiday period; brutally flogged, denied a part of even the kitchen's festivities and locked in his bedroom, he is as isolated as he was on that lonely night when he first arrived at Wuthering Heights.

Rejected by the inmates of both Wuthering Heights and Thrushcross Grange, is it surprising that Heathcliff rejects the values of the society around him? His final alienation takes place when he overhears Catherine telling Nelly that she intends to marry Edgar Linton because it would degrade her to marry Heathcliff; he does not overhear, however, her passionate declaration that:

> Every Linton on the face of the earth might melt into nothing, before I could consent to forsake Heathcliff! . . . My love for Linton is like the foliage in the woods. Time will change it, I'm well aware, as winter changes the trees. My love for Heathcliff resembles the external rocks beneath - a source of little visible delight, but necessary. (Chapter 9)

It is, in fact, his final acceptance, the only acceptance he has ever wished for, but it has come too late; by the time these words are uttered he has already left Wuthering Heights. When he returns three years later he has achieved one of the Victorian ideals - he has become a 'self-made man' - but it is a hollow victory, for Catherine is already married to Edgar and by every moral standard of the time beyond Heathcliff's reach. We may notice that at no time does Catherine contemplate leaving her husband, for whilst she continues to live at Thrushcross Grange she may be near to Heathcliff, whereas to return to Wuthering Heights is out of the question. Besides, Edgar is a gentle and loving husband able to lavish every luxury on her and Catherine is selfish enough to prefer the elegant life he can offer her. Isabella, of course, leaves Heathcliff but not to fall into the arms of another man and, in any case, her situation is very different.

The first part of the novel ends with the death of Catherine and Heathcliff's agonised understanding of his own isolation. The loss of love results in the loss of humanity. Whether Catherine's love could have brought Heathcliff salvation we cannot know, but without it he is in hell. The second part of the novel reverses the movement of the first, though with a different set of characters. Hindley dies, ruined, and Heathcliff revenges himself further by demeaning Hareton, bringing him up, as he himself had been brought up, as an illiterate boor. Yet a strange kinship blossoms between the two; Heathcliff never physically ill-treats the lad and Hareton repays him with a dogged affection. When love begins to grow between Cathy and Hareton it at first appears to replicate the situation of Catherine and Heathcliff in the earlier generation: 'Your love,' Heathcliff tells Cathy, 'will make him an outcast, and a beggar' (Chapter 33). Their love continues to develop, however, a calmer, kindlier, less passionate love than that of their predecessors and, for Heathcliff, Hareton becomes an *alter ego*, a second self:

> a personification of my youth, not a human being . . . [his] aspect was the ghost of my immortal love, of my wild endeavours to hold my right, my degradation, my pride, my happiness, and my anguish. (Chapter 33)

To destroy Hareton's hopes was like destroying his own. In the love of the two younger people he finds a kind of vicarious fulfilment which seems to bring him closer to Catherine.

Does he walk the moors with her in death? It would be a romantic ending to a novel where love has struggled to triumph under burdens of misery and despair, even though the prosaic Lockwood cannot 'imagine unquiet slumbers, for the sleepers in that quiet earth' (Chapter 34).

So much for the plot but a good novel amounts to more than its story. What is *Wuthering Heights* about? What are its main themes? And has it any relevance for us today?

3.2 THEMES

On the simplest level *Wuthering Heights* is the story of base ingratitude, of a waif who grows up to return evil for good but this is not merely simple, it is simplistic. The novel is a complicated lattice of themes which work on several levels at once. It is about love and jealousy and revenge, about loss and desire; it is about selfishness and self-willedness, about cruelty, violence and fear, about the evils of drunkenness, about the bringing up of children and education; it is about books and religion, about freedom and subjugation, about untamed nature and the conventions of society, about happiness and misery, about alienation, about sickness and death; it is about the strange and the supernatural, about the homely and the familiar; and finally, it is about a spiritual accord which defies separation and death to achieve reconciliation in a life beyond the grave.

Love
Despite the richness of ideas in the novel, or perhaps because of it, critics have found it peculiarly difficult to agree on the main themes. Certainly

the theme of love, particularly the love between Catherine and Heathcliff, is central. The deep, engrossing passion they show for each other has in it a spiritual quality which goes far beyond the normal personal plane of romantic love. Only by understanding how their personalities are sub-sumed into each other are we able to appreciate the agony of their separation. When Catherine tells Nelly that she intends to marry Edgar, Nelly suggests that it is because 'he is handsome, and young, and cheerful, and rich, and loves you' (Chapter 9); Catherine, however, adds a further reason, for she believes that through her marriage to Edgar she will be able to raise Heathcliff out of his degradation. She goes on to try to explain to Nelly the dilemma of her feelings for Heathcliff, whom she loves, 'not because he's handsome . . . but because he's more myself than I am'. She struggles to put into words her empathy with him and in doing so she delineates a love very like the Christian view of holy love. (Compare 'God is love; and he that dwelleth in love dwelleth in God, and God in him.' (I John 4.16).) She sees Heathcliff as 'one who comprehends [that is, 'includes', not 'understands'] in his person my feelings to Edgar and myself' and suggests that her continued being is entirely dependent on him:

> . . . my great thought in living is himself. If all else perished, and *he* remained, I should still continue to be; and if all else remained, and he were annihilated, the universe would turn to a mighty stranger. I should not seem a part of it. . . . Nelly, I *am* Heathcliff – he's always, always in my mind – not as a pleasure, any more than I am always a pleasure to myself – but as my own being . . .

Ironically, even whilst she is speaking, the presence of Heathcliff is with-drawn from her. When he runs away she is left desolate and we should notice that, despite the disbelief of the others, Catherine *knows* that he will not return. We should not be surprised at her subsequent mental breakdown, for Heathcliff's disappearance alienates her from the world, turning the universe 'to a mighty stranger'.

Nelly passes over the next three years of her narrative in a couple of pages; Catherine's marriage to Edgar at the end of that period is briefly referred to but it is almost as if time for Catherine had ceased to exist; we know little more of her life during Heathcliff's absence than we know of his. Only after his return does she express to Nelly the anguish she has felt, 'Oh, I've endured very, very bitter misery, Nelly!' (Chapter 10). Significantly, she sees Heathcliff's reappearance in the light of a religious experience, an event which 'has reconciled me to God, and humanity!'

An awareness of Catherine's emotional state during that time of sep-aration will help us to understand Heathcliff's desolation at her death;

part of him (which he calls his 'soul') has died with Catherine. 'Oh, God!' he cries out, 'It is unutterable! I *cannot* live without my life! I *cannot* live without my soul!' (Chapter 16). Again, it is a deeply-felt emotion, akin to spiritual loss. Throughout the rest of the novel he seeks to be reunited with Catherine and he continually presents his search in religious terms: he prays her spirit to return to him (Chapter 29); he feels 'unspeakably consoled' by the sense of her presence (Chapter 29); a few days before his death he tells Nelly, 'I am within sight of my heaven' and, a little later, after talking of his happiness and how his 'soul's bliss' is killing his body, he claims 'I have nearly attained *my* heaven' (Chapter 34). He appears finally to have achieved redemption through suffering.

The theme of love is reflected also in the lives of some of the lesser characters. Hindley, who appears to have little feeling for any of his own family, is a devoted husband, fulfilling every whim of his wife, Frances. They, too, however, are separated by death and, left alone, Hindley gives himself up entirely to drunken dissipation. Edgar's love for Catherine and Cathy's for young Linton also end in separation through death, so that we may perhaps see the main theme not as love, but as the frustration of love. Only Cathy and Hareton seem set to have a happy and successful marriage for their tribulations have occurred in the period before their courtship.

Revenge

Another powerful theme in the novel is that of revenge; it is linked from the beginning to the theme of love, for when Hindley takes control of the household at Wuthering Heights he remembers how Heathcliff had usurped his position in his father's love and decides to revenge himself. Thus the cycle of revenge begins, for the repeated indignities heaped upon Heathcliff make him determined to 'pay Hindley back'; he tells Nelly:

> I don't care how long I wait, if I can only do it, at last. I hope he will not die before I do! ... I only wish I knew the best way! Let me alone, and I'll plan it out ... (Chapter 7)

It is not until later that Catherine's marriage persuades Heathcliff to extend his revenge to the Lintons. So Hareton is degraded to pay for Heathcliff's degradation; a Cathy is forcibly married to a Heathcliff to make up for Catherine and Heathcliff's separation; Heathcliff becomes master of Wuthering Heights, where he was once treated worse than a servant, and owner of Thrushcross Grange, which had been responsible for taking Catherine from him. But this Old Testament justice is finally resolved in New Testament grace: Hareton is 'raised' by Cathy, just as Catherine had once hoped to raise Heathcliff; Linton dies, paving the way for love to blossom between Cathy and Hareton; and finally, Heathcliff is redeemed through love and suffering, his spirit to be reunited with Catherine's spirit after death, and Wuthering Heights and Thrushcross Grange return to the heirs of the Earnshaws and the Lintons.

The Supernatural

The spiritual element which seems to run through the themes of both love and revenge is further extended in the more general treatment of the supernatural. The novel is concerned not only with life in its physical manifestations but also with something beyond the physical. There are early hints of this metaphysical thread in the language of the first few chapters: 'fiends . . . magically . . . devil . . . herd of possessed swine (Chapter 1); 'ministering angel . . . beneficent fairy . . . good fairy . . . devil's name . . . Black Art . . . modelled in wax and clay . . . little witch . . . ghost . . . cursing' (Chapter 2). Such random references, however, are merely a preparation for a much more carefully structured supernatural contribution to the novel as a whole.

First, we should observe that the actual narration of the tale is on several levels at once and the first of these is that of the fairy story or legend. It is a tale told by the fireside on a winter's evening by an elderly woman, the family nurse, sitting and narrating as she sews. Fleeting echoes of childhood fairy tales are recalled as she proceeds. Mr Earnshaw's journey to Liverpool and his promise to bring back presents for the three children left at home resemble the journey and promise of the merchant in 'Beauty and the Beast'. What the merchant brings back is one red rose, symbol of the Beast to whom he has to give his younger daughter in recompense. What Mr Earnshaw brings home is 'a dirty, ragged, black-haired child' (Chapter 4) who wins his daughter's heart. In the fairy tale the Beast is transformed into a handsome prince and this idea is echoed in the novel where Heathcliff appears to be the Beast's equivalent.

Fairy-tale transformations are constantly taking place: Hindley returns after his three years at college thinner, paler and speaking and dressing 'quite differently' (Chapter 6); Catherine comes back from Thrushcross Grange not the 'wild, hatless little savage' she had been earlier but a beautiful and elegant young lady (Chapter 7); even more significant are Nelly's comments to Heathcliff when she wants to tidy him up after Catherine's return home:

> You're fit for a prince in disguise. Who knows, but your father was Emperor of China, and your mother an Indian queen, each of them able to buy up, with one week's income, Wuthering Heights and Thrushcross Grange together? And you were kidnapped by wicked sailors, and brought to England. (Chapter 7)

In fact, when Heathcliff returns after his three-year absence (and notice how both he and Hindley are away for three years – three is itself a fairy number), Nelly talks of his 'transformation' (Chapter 10); when Isabella goes to Wuthering Heights after her marriage she is transformed from her former elegance into a slut (Chapter 14); Hareton is transformed from a coarse bumpkin into a personable young man; the final transformation in the book is that which Lockwood observes when he returns after his stay in London (Chapter 32).

Though the tale of 'Beauty and the Beast' is the most obvious fairy-tale source, there are many other echoes from myth and legend to which fleeting reference is made. Whether such was Emily Brontë's intention or not, these serve to enlarge the story by drawing in emotional over-tones from outside the bounds of the actual plot. For instance, in Chapter 12, early in what proves to be Catherine's final illness, she believes that she is back at Wuthering Heights and she imagines she sees a face looking at her; it is her own face reflected in the mirror but as Nelly tries to convince her of this the clock strikes midnight; when Catherine cries out, 'Myself! . . . and the clock is striking twelve!' we realise that her 'Cinderella dream' has dissolved, though she is not Cinders but the poor little rich girl whose dream of happiness with her prince in disguise, i.e. Heathcliff, has vanished at the stroke of twelve. Again, much later in the story, when Heathcliff has tricked Nelly and Cathy into entering Wuthering Heights, we may well recall the legend of Proserpina and Pluto as Cathy declares, 'I wouldn't eat or drink here, if I were starving' (Chapter 27).

This legend, belonging to both Roman and Greek tradition, tells the story of Proserpina, daughter of Ceres (Mother Earth), who was seized by Pluto, god of the Underworld, and taken to his kingdom; once there she refused to eat or drink but Pluto finally persuaded her to eat six pomegranate seeds. Because of this, Zeus decreed that she had to spend six months of every year in the Underworld. It is the myth of the seasons; whilst Proserpina is below the ground her mother Ceres neglects to care for plants, animals or mankind. The faint echo of the old myth equates Heathcliff with the dark king of the Underworld.

On another plane, however, a realistic story superimposes itself upon the fairy tale but the two are so skilfully fused that the reader accepts supernatural events as part of the natural world. The most striking instance of this is the appearance of Lockwood's little ghost, for she is a substantial flesh and blood ghost whose reality is confirmed for us by Lockwood's gratuitous act of cruelty as he rubs her wrist across the jagged broken glass of the window (Chapter 3). In the moment in which her blood flows down and soaks the bed-clothes the reality of this other world of ghosts and spirits is established for us. As the novel proceeds we do not doubt that

Heathcliff, more passionate and more imaginative than Lockwood, has glimpses of that other world and of Catherine; and certainly, just before her death Catherine believes that she is escaping, not into nothingness, but into a new sphere 'incomparably beyond and above you all' (Chapter 15).

The prosaic Lockwood believes at the end that no one 'could ever imagine unquiet slumbers, for the sleepers in that quiet earth' but the whole tenor of the story suggests the possibility of Heathcliff and Catherine, happy together at last, walking the moors around Wuthering Heights in the spiritual union not allowed to them on earth.

However, the novel is not an overtly religious one and if we ask whether there is a moral in it for us today we may well find the question difficult to answer. Certainly, we may learn of the evils of drunkenness, of the ill effects of corporal punishment, of the psychological traumas brought on by the deprivation of love. We may learn, too, that hate and jealousy are destructive, that money and education do not necessarily bring happiness. More positively, we can see that love fulfilled has the power to change lives. Yet Emily Brontë is not a 'moral novelist' in the Victorian sense; she sets out not to teach us a lesson but to tell us a story; in doing so she is not concerned with laws or politics or religion but with man. Heathcliff may rely on law or the corruption of law to acquire the titles to both Thrushcross Grange and Wuthering Heights; old Joseph may use religion to conduct his pernicious campaigns of hate; but in all the multitudinous themes of the novel what we are really looking at is the condition of man and for Emily Brontë man is not contained in this world but continually reaches outward: ' ... surely', Catherine tells Nelly, 'you and everybody have a notion that there is, or should be an existence of yours beyond you' (Chapter 9). The novel is concerned with Heathcliff and Catherine, with Edgar, Isabella, Cathy and Hareton and through them with the themes of love, of separation, of alienation and of revenge. In these principal characters we are brought face to face with naked human emotions which we may be unable to sympathise with but which we, nevertheless, understand. However, there is a mystic element in the novel which overlays the incidents of the plot; the spiritual dimension is implicit in the events and we are left with the uneasy feeling that we may have participated in a profound religious experience which we do not fully understand.

3.3 NARRATION AND THE USE OF TIME

The narration of *Wuthering Heights* is skilfully contrived in order to allow the reader to see multiple perspectives within a first person account. The main problem with first person narratives is their subjectivity: the reader observes the tale through the narrow point of view of the teller of the tale; what he does not see, the reader may not see; what he does not know is denied to the reader also; moreover, the characters in the story are viewed through his eyes alone. Emily Brontë has overcome this problem by placing within Lockwood's narration a number of other narratives which flesh out the bare bones of the tale and show the characters in varying lights.

The story starts in 1771, though the novel itself begins some thirty years later, in November 1801. Lockwood's first journal entry shows no sense of being in the middle of a story and we ourselves do not realise that this is the case until the third chapter. Meanwhile, we have already been given two conflicting views of Heathcliff. Lockwood's first reaction to him is that he is a 'capital fellow! . . . a dark skinned gypsy, in aspect, in dress, and manners a gentleman'; the events of Chapter 2, however, make Lockwood see him as an 'unmannerly wretch'.

The first interpolated narrative is that of Catherine's diary; it takes us back to 1777, just after the death of old Mr Earnshaw. Now we see Heathcliff in a quite different perspective, not the proud, domineering character that Lockwood has seen but a child, oppressed and ill-treated. Catherine's sympathy for him prepares us to accept the third view of him which follows Lockwood's nightmare when Heathcliff is shown in emotional agony, sobbing in 'an uncontrollable passion of tears'. Lockwood cannot understand the outburst but much later in the novel, though earlier in point of time by seventeen years, we shall recall this incident when, after Catherine's death, Nelly watches Heathcliff and thinks 'Poor wretch . . . you have a heart and nerves the same as your brother men! Why should you be anxious to conceal them?' (Chapter 16).

Lockwood's outer narrative then has already briefly contained a second view of part of the story before either he or we are in any way aware of its significance. Taken together these introductory chapters have aroused our expectations and whetted our appetite more than any chronological telling of the tale could have done. We want to know what has happened to transform the bullied and neglected boy into the harsh and dour owner of Wuthering Heights and Thrushcross Grange; we want to know who the little ghost-child is and why she rouses him to so much passion; we want to know how Heathcliff came to have a son who married 'the beneficent fairy' of Lockwood's vision and then died, leaving her in the unloving care of her father-in-law.

As an uninvolved outsider, Lockwood is able to give us an objective view of what he sees, always coloured, of course, by his own personality. Thus the plot of the novel begins with a picture of life at Wuthering Heights as it would appear to an onlooker; but things are not always what they seem. To get the details of the story it is necessary to hear it from one who has observed it from the beginning. The narrative transition to Nelly's tale is completely credible. Tired and sick after his unfortunate experiences of the preceding two days, Lockwood begins to ask his house-keeper the very questions that we ourselves have been asking; he is so intrigued with the bits of information proffered that he begs Nelly to tell him the whole story: 'Before I came to live here, she commenced . . . ' Her opening words have a fairy-tale quality; the original narrator now becomes an auditor. The atmosphere is one of quiet ordinariness; it is an after-supper tale, told beside the fire on a chilly winter's night, the teller sewing whilst she speaks, the listener swallowing down a basin of hot gruel and passively absorbing the strange story which unfolds itself.

Nelly Dean is an excellent choice for narrator: in the Earnshaw family, but not of it, she is a keen observer of the life around her; she is the confi-dante of several members of the family; at the same time she is able to gossip with the servants and the local people; she is intelligent and well-read, though not well-educated. Above all, she is neither a completely dis-interested outsider nor a main participant in the action. With Nelly, then, the perspective of the tale shifts once again. She takes us back to a time six years earlier than Catherine's diary, to the summer of 1771. Thus we have approached the story in chronologically reverse order – first, the events of the present of the greater part of the novel, 1801, then a brief glance at the childhood of Catherine and Heathcliff in 1777 and now, with Nelly's narration, the beginning of it all.

We are constantly reminded that we are not the only auditors of the tale, for Nelly is conscious of Lockwood's presence; she interrupts herself several times to enquire after his comfort and occasionally asks him questions to draw him back into the narration. In Chapter 31 he again becomes the narrator as, now fully recovered from his sickness, he prepares to go away from Thrushcross Grange. When he finally departs for London we are left in suspense for, without a listener, Nelly cannot go on with her tale. In the following chapter, however, Lockwood resumes the story. It begins with the date 1802 and takes place some eight months after the end of the previous chapter when he returns to the neighbourhood. Nelly is once more called upon to tell him what has happened in the interim and the novel ends where it began with Lockwood the principal narrator returning to Thrushcross Grange after a visit to Wuthering Heights. Before he goes away, however, he lingers in the churchyard beside the graves of the principal protagonists, trying to reassert his sense of normality which has been sorely strained through his incursions into the lives of the Earnshaws and the Lintons.

As Nelly is a first-person narrator she can relate only what she sees and knows or what other characters tell her. Thus Hindley's absence at college and Heathcliff's three-year absence are not enlarged upon because

44

neither of the men chooses to inform Nelly about his life at that time. On the other hand, incidents which are told to Nelly are given to the reader in the direct words of the teller: Heathcliff tells of his and Catherine's adventure at Thrushcross Grange (Chapter 6); Catherine tells her her innermost thoughts when she declares her love for Heathcliff (Chapter 9); Isabella tells how she and Hindley attempted to lock Heathcliff out of Wuthering Heights (Chapter 17); Heathcliff gives his own account of this same incident (Chapter 29); Cathy describes her illicit visits to Wuthering Heights (Chapter 24); Zillah tells of Cathy's life at Wuthering Heights after her marriage to Linton (Chapter 30). Additionally, Isabella recounts in a letter to Nelly her own experiences of life as Heathcliff's wife (Chapter 13). These multiple narratives enable us to gain an overall view of the story and allow us, through observing a number of different subjective viewpoints, to look more objectively at the events and the characters.

Figure 3.1 *List of dates*

1500 Wuthering Heights built by a Hareton Earnshaw
1757 Birth of Hindley Earnshaw and probably of Ellen Dean
1762 Birth of Edgar Linton
1765 Birth of Catherine Earnshaw
1766 Birth of Isabella Linton
1771 Mr Earnshaw brings Heathcliff to Wuthering Heights
1773 Death of Mrs Earnshaw
1774 Hindley sent away to college
1777 Marriage of Hindley and Frances
     October: Death of Mr Earnshaw; return of Hindley
     November: Catherine goes to stay at Thrushcross Grange
     Christmas: Catherine returns home to Wuthering Heights
1778 *June:* Birth of Hareton
     Autumn: Death of Frances
1780 Heathcliff runs away
     Deaths of Mr and Mrs Linton
1783 *April:* Marriage of Catherine and Edgar
     September: Heathcliff returns
1784 *January:* Marriage of Heathcliff and Isabella
     20 March: Birth of Cathy; death of Catherine
     September: Death of Hindley; birth of Linton Heathcliff
1797 *July:* Death of Isabella; Cathy visits Wuthering Heights and meets
          Hareton; Linton brought to Thrushcross Grange and then
          taken to Wuthering Heights
1800 *20 March:* Cathy meets Heathcliff and sees Linton again
1801 *August:* Marriage of Cathy and Linton
     September: Death of Edgar
     October: Death of Linton
     November: Lockwood goes to Thrushcross Grange and visits
          Wuthering Heights
1802 *January:* Lockwood returns to London
     May: Death of Heathcliff
     September: Lockwood returns to Thrushcross Grange
1803 *1 January:* Marriage of Cathy and Hareton

If we move from consideration of the narrators to that of what is being narrated we see an equally skilful handling: Emily Brontë demonstrates that she knows when to expand and when to summarise. Her thirty-four chapters deal with the events of almost as many years and the pace of the novel varies according to her material. Sometimes a single incident is probed with meticulous detail, several pages or even one or more chapters being dedicated to it; sometimes the events of weeks, months or years are passed over with no more than a brief reference: 'Cathy stayed at Thrushcross Grange five weeks, till Christmas. By that time her ankle was thoroughly cured, and her manners much improved' (Chapter 7).

One of the most fascinating aspects of *Wuthering Heights* is Emily Brontë's handling of time. The present or 'now' of the novel is a little under a year from November 1801 to September 1802. During this period the story passes through thirty-one years of chronological time and, despite the fact that (apart from the '1500' over the door at Wuthering Heights) only three dates are mentioned in the whole book (the third is 1778 at the end of Chapter 7), every birth, death or marriage and practically every event that takes place can be dated fairly precisely, invariably to the year, frequently to the month or day. Look at Figure 3.1. For confirmation of this you should read C.P. Sanger's *The Structure of Wuthering Heights* (1926), in which he establishes the reliability of Brontë's dating. (By reference to our Computer Centre I was recently able to resolve simply his uncertainty as to whether Catherine died and Cathy was born on a Monday as the novel suggests, or on a Saturday as Sanger believed. 20 March 1784 was, in fact, a Saturday).

The story starts *in medias res*, that is, 'in the middle'; or perhaps it would be more correct to say, almost at the end, for it is only the final resolution of the plot that takes place later than the events of the first three and a half chapters. Once the chronological story is under way we are quickly drawn into its atmosphere; however, lest we should forget that it is a tale being told to an independent observer who has by chance become involved in the final stages of the events, we are constantly referred back to Lockwood. This serves also to remind us that three of the characters Nelly is discussing are still alive and, apparently rather incongruously, are living together at Wuthering Heights. The first return to 1801 occurs at the end of Chapter 7 after the disastrous Christmas celebrations when Catherine had returned from Thrushcross Grange; it brings us down from a high emotional plane to the calm of the novel's present; when Nelly resumes it is summer and she is reporting the birth of Hareton. The second interruption is at the end of Chapter 9 when Heathcliff has disappeared, Catherine and Edgar have just been married and, with Nelly, have gone to live at Thrushcross Grange. The third (Chapter 14) precedes the events leading up to the death of Catherine

Figure 3.2 *A graph showing the time sequence within the novel*

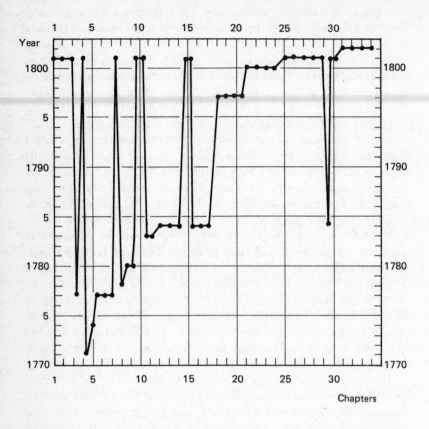

and the birth of Cathy. Each of these interruptions occurs at a point when there is a powerful build-up of emotions in the reader; they serve momentarily to lower the tension, thus allowing the next build-up to begin from a slightly lower point.

The other dramatic switch in time is the flashback in Chapter 29, when Heathcliff tells Nelly what he did on the night of Catherine's funeral. As he finishes this account by describing from his point of view how he returned to Wuthering Heights to find that Isabella and Hindley had locked him out, we realise with a shock of recognition that this is the same incident which Isabella had recounted to Nelly in Chapter 17. The brutality of that event, whilst not vindicated, is somewhat mitigated by the knowledge of the agonised state of Heathcliff's emotions at the time. Once more we are given a shifting perspective and we find that our sympathy with Heathcliff, which had almost disappeared in more recent chapters, is renewed. See Figure 3.2.

3.4 THE TWO HOUSES

Though the novel begins in Thrushcross Grange as Lockwood writes his journal, the subject of his thoughts is Wuthering Heights; thus the two houses are linked together from the outset. The world of the novel is centred on them and the geographical setting is narrowly circumscribed. The nearby village of Gimmerton is a point of reference but has no part in the plot of the novel. The milestone at the crossroads points northwards to Wuthering Heights, south-west to Thrushcross Grange, eastwards to Gimmerton and to the west the road branches off over the moor (Chapter 11). Thrushcross Grange and Wuthering Heights are four miles apart (Chapter 2); beyond the Heights, Penistone Crags are a further one and a half miles (Chapter 18). Emily Brontë, it is clear, was as precise about the topography of the novel as she was about the chronology.

In the first chapter Lockwood gives a very detailed description of Wuthering Heights as it appears to him in the November of 1801. Outside, the garden and surroundings have an air of neglect, 'grass grows up between the flags, and cattle are the only hedge-cutters'. The chained gate signifies a lack of welcome, reinforced by the fortress-like appearance of the house itself with its 'narrow windows . . . deeply set in the wall' and 'corners defended with large jutting stones'. Lockwood is not allowed to dwell on the lighter side of the architecture – the 'grotesque carving . . . of crumbling griffins, and shameless little boys' – for he is swiftly ushered through the door. He does observe, however, the name 'Hareton Earnshaw' and the date 1500, though its significance seems scarcely to register with him when in Chapter 2 Hareton announces his name. The inhabitants of the house are as unwelcoming as its exterior; Heathcliff precedes Lockwood up the path 'sullenly' and Joseph responds to orders 'in an undertone of peevish displeasure'.

Inside, however, there is an atmosphere of homely well-being; the 'house' or family sitting-room is bright and cheerful. An oak dresser houses pewter and silver dishes and jugs which reflect the light and heat from the fire; in an arch beneath is a recess where a pointer bitch lies with her puppies. Above the fireplace itself is a collection of guns and, on a high ledge, 'three gaudily painted canisters'. Above all this is the roof with its struts and beams fully visible except where piles of home-made oatcakes are standing on wooden frames or where 'legs of beef, mutton, and ham' are hanging. The floor is white stone and the furniture is heavy, primitive and functional; as Lockwood observes, it would be well-suited to the home of any northern farmer of the time.

But Emily Brontë never uses words gratuitously; Lockwood's observations serve more than a descriptive purpose, for the condition of the house at different times in the tale reflects the fortunes of its inhabitants. Years before Lockwood's visit to Wuthering Heights, in 1777 at the time of Mr Earnshaw's death and early in Hindley's marriage, Frances expresses her delight in 'the white floor, and huge glowing fire-place, at the pewter dishes, and delf-case, and dog-kennel' (Chapter 6). Until this time the house has been cared for, mainly by Nelly as house-keeper. When Catherine and Edgar marry and Nelly goes with them to Thrushcross Grange, Wuthering Heights is left entirely in the hands of Hindley and it is completely neglected. Thus, after her marriage to Heathcliff, Isabella writes to Nelly describing her new home:

> There was a great fire, and that was all the light in the huge apart-ment, whose floor had grown a uniform grey; and the once brilliant pewter dishes, which used to attract my gaze when I was a girl, partook of a similar obscurity, created by tarnish and dust. (Chapter 13)

The room becomes a symbol of her despair and when Nelly visits her she comments that Isabella 'already partook of the pervading spirit of neglect which encompassed her' (Chapter 14). After Hindley's death, however, a kind of uneasy peace descends on Wuthering Heights; Heathcliff employs a housekeeper again and when Nelly visits in 1797 she comments that 'the house, inside, had regained its ancient aspect of comfort under female management' (Chapter 18). The Heights was then probably much as Lockwood saw it on his first visit in 1801 but when he returns in September 1802 he observes major changes, not in the comfort of the interior but in the welcoming air of the exterior: the gate is no longer chained; the doors and windows are open and he is greeted by the scent of flowers as he walks up the path (Chapter 32).

By comparison (though it is there that the story is told by Nelly and written in his journal by Lockwood) we learn considerably less about Thrushcross Grange. In the early chapters Lockwood returns there as to a place of refuge after his visits to the Heights. From his comments we learn that the Grange has extensive grounds – it is two miles from the gate to the house (Chapter 3) – and that the house itself is somewhat superior to Wuthering Heights; whilst the latter is a fairly typical farm-house, the Grange is one of the 'big houses' of the neighbourhood. Our first real view of Thrushcross Grange is given by Heathcliff to Nelly after he and Catherine have been caught looking in the window.

Heathcliff is clearly impressed with what he sees and describes with wonder the Linton's drawing-room. The room is lit by a sparkling chandelier, 'a shower of glass-drops hanging in silver chains...and shimmering with little soft tapers'; the light is reflected downwards from a 'pure white ceiling bordered by gold'. In contrast to the white stone floor and the green and black chairs of Wuthering Heights, Heathcliff sees a 'splendid place carpeted with crimson, and crimson-covered chairs and tables' (Chapter 6). Yet within the elegant room Edgar and Isabella are quarrelling and crying; Thrushcross Grange is as much the home of human emotions as is Wuthering Heights, though the emotions displayed are emasculated, petty jealousy and spite replacing the passions of love and hate so robustly expressed in the more primitive house.

When Nelly becomes housekeeper there our knowledge of the Grange is gradually extended, yet we never get to know it as intimately as we know Wuthering Heights. The most detailed interior description is that given by Heathcliff and quoted above, though various rooms, such as library and parlour are mentioned and in her final illness Catherine has a room next to the parlour 'fixed up' for her use (Chapter 13). There is quite a large staff at Thrushcross Grange but unlike Joseph they are kept in their place so, apart from Nelly, we learn nothing of them; at various times, however, she mentions 'one of the maids' (thus indicating that there are several), a coachman and two gardeners; Heathcliff speaks of 'footmen'; there is a porter's lodge – and presumably, therefore, a porter – at the main gate and Nelly herself is the housekeeper. Every reference to the furnishings suggests comfort; Catherine has a featherpillow on her bed and a large mirror in her room (Chapter 12) and in Chapter 17 'an easy chair' is mentioned. It is not surprising that, at the end of the novel, Nelly is looking forward to leaving Wuthering Heights, which she calls 'this grim house', and going back to Thrushcross Grange.

Throughout the novel Wuthering Heights is seen not only as the home of life in the raw, of unbridled emotions and passions, but also as the place of general abundance. Food is always plentiful; meals are constantly being prepared and eaten; immense, comforting fires always fill the grate; the basic human needs of food and warmth are more than sufficiently supplied. Only once do we enter the main sitting-room of Wuthering Heights to find that the fire is nearly out; that is when Nelly and Cathy visit Linton during Heathcliff's absence (Chapter 23); the dying fire is a sign of the servant's neglect; with Nelly's arrival it is soon replenished but the dying boy who sits beside it cannot so easily be revitalised.

Life at Thrushcross Grange, on the other hand, is cold and inhibited. Lockwood is driven to his second visit to the Heights by the lack of a fire in his study, though when he returns there after the ordeal of his nightmare in Catherine's bedroom he is warmed by a 'cheerful fire and smoking coffee' (Chapter 3). Meals are rarely mentioned and food is either dainty or frugal; so Lockwood eats gruel to ward off the cold (Chapter 4); Catherine has a plate of cakes tipped into her lap and is given a 'tumbler of negus' (Chapter 6). In Chapter 12 Nelly prepares 'some tea and dry toast' for her.

It is significant that in the first generation the fiery, passionate characters belong to Wuthering Heights, whilst those who are colder and more restrained come from Thrushcross Grange. Lord David Cecil in his essay on Emily Brontë in *Early Victorian Novelists* describes the families respectively as 'children of the storm' and 'children of calm'. If in the second generation distinctions become blurred, it is because Cathy, Linton and Hareton combine the qualities of both their parents. There will be further discussion of this point in the section on characters.

Many critics have commented on the balance and symmetry in the novel. The Earnshaws and the Lintons live respectively at Wuthering Heights and Thrushcross Grange (see Figure 3.3). At the commencement of the plot Mr and Mrs Earnshaw and Mr and Mrs Linton are all alive and each household has two children, one boy and one girl, Hindley and Catherine, Edgar and Isabella; two outsiders are introduced, one male and one female, Heathcliff and Frances. When they grow up Earnshaws and Lintons are linked through the marriage of Catherine and Edgar, whilst Hindley

Figure 3.3   *The two houses and the two families*

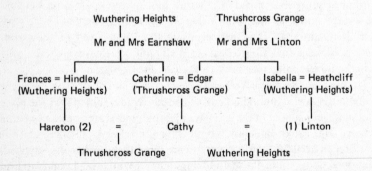

marries Frances and Isabella marries Heathcliff. The children of these unions – Cathy, Hareton and Linton – are, between them, the heirs of both houses. When they grow up Cathy marries in turn, first Linton Heathcliff and then Hareton Earnshaw, Heathcliff's natural and spiritual heirs. With Linton she moves from Thrushcross Grange to Wuthering Heights; with Hareton, at the end of the novel, she is about to move from Wuthering Heights to Thrushcross Grange. Thus, the intricate pattern of relationships is perfected and the two houses revert jointly to the heirs of both the families.

4 TECHNIQUES

4.1 CHARACTERS AND CHARACTERISATION

In keeping with the narrow geographical confines of the novel, the number of characters is small. The two households of Earnshaw and Linton are a world in themselves and we know practically nothing of the lives of the people of Gimmerton, let alone those from farther afield. Inevitably when discussing other aspects of the novel quite a lot has been said about the characters. However, it is useful to look at some of them more closely.

Heathcliff
Heathcliff is an extremely enigmatic figure. In a formal sense he lacks identity: his parentage and nationality are unknown, as is also his precise age. Though named after an Earnshaw son 'who died in childhood' (Chapter 4), he never becomes an Earnshaw; his single name – Heathcliff – serves, as Nelly states, 'both for Christian and surname' (Chapter 4), so she calls him 'Heathcliff' as a boy and 'Mr Heathcliff' as a man. Yet it appears that he was christened (Chapter 4) and when he dies he is buried in sanctified ground in Gimmerton kirkyard (Chapter 34) where his headstone bears no other inscription but 'Heathcliff' and the date of his death (Chapter 33).

From the outset his origin is a mystery. Old Mr Earnshaw finds him starving and homeless on the streets of Liverpool and brings him back to Wuthering Heights; we might notice that in describing the evening and morning following Mr Earnshaw's return Nelly consistently calls Heathcliff 'it', as though he were animal, not human; only when she comes back from her temporary banishment to find that he has been given a name does she deign to give him the dignity of a human being by using the personal pronouns 'he' and 'him'. Twice in the novel Heathcliff disappears. The first time, when he is about sixteen years old, he appears to have gone for good; no one knows anything of him during the time of his absence yet, after three years, he returns, not a dirty, unkempt vagabond but a gentleman. His second disappearance is for two months with Isabella Linton; during this time all we learn of the couple is that they are married; even in her long letter to Nelly (Chapter 13) Isabella says nothing of their life together prior to their return to Wuthering Heights.

The sense of mystery is heightened by the mode of Heathcliff's death; he tells Nelly that he feels 'a strange change approaching' (Chapter 33); the first sign of this is that he has lost the will to destroy his old enemies. He is restless and spends his time wandering about; he does not sleep; he eats nothing. Yet he is clearly experiencing some excess of joy: 'I'm too happy, and yet I'm not happy enough', he explains, 'My soul's bliss kills my body, but does not satisfy itself' (Chapter 34). When he is found dead in Catherine's old bedroom Dr Kenneth is unable to state a cause of death and though Nelly conceals the fact that he has not eaten for four days it is scarcely likely that a strong healthy man in the prime of life (he was about thirty-seven) would die of starvation in such a short time. Thus we have to look for another explanation of his death but there *is* none, at least, no rational explanation. He leaves Wuthering Heights as he came – an enigma.

Is he, in fact, a human being or a creature from another sphere? A demon? Or a devil? Because of the strong supernatural element in the novel it is necessary at least to look at this idea. Nelly, who has known him for most of his life, is responsible for much of the speculation about his origin and identity. Not only does she suggest to him the possibility of a romantic heritage, that he might be a son of the Emperor of China and an Indian queen (Chapter 7) but she suggests to us, the readers, a more sinister lineage: 'Is he a ghoul, or a vampire?. . . where did he come from, the little dark thing, harboured by a good man to his bane?' (Chapter 34). Physically, Heathcliff displays features often attributed to the Devil: in the very first chapter Lockwood observes his black eyes and dark skin; the motif of darkness is constantly used in reference to him. When Mr Earnshaw first brings him to Wuthering Heights he offers him to the family as 'a gift of God; though it's as dark almost as if it came from the devil' (Chapter 4). Nelly describes his eyes as a 'couple of black fiends' and compares them to 'devil's spies' (Chapter 7) and Isabella talks of them as the 'clouded windows of hell' (Chapter 17). It is not surprising that when he returns from his three-year absence with black whiskers and lowering brows Nelly remembers him by his eyes 'deepset and singular' (Chapter 10). The devil-like role is principally one imposed upon him by the superstitious Nelly; she has heard Hindley as a boy call him an 'imp of Satan' (Chapter 4) but when they have all grown to maturity she begins to be obsessed with a superstitious fear of him so that when she goes to visit Hindley one day and Heathcliff comes to the door she runs away 'feeling as scared as if I had raised a goblin' (Chapter 11). The goblin image remains in her mind to terrify her during Heathcliff's last days so that she has 'neither the nerve nor the will' to stay alone with him (Chapter 34). 'I believe you think me a fiend,' he comments to her and to Cathy he remarks, ' . . . to you, I've made myself worse than the devil.'

Were he a devil, or a possessed soul, we could perhaps more easily understand his cruelty, his violence and his desire for revenge; we could understand his relentless destruction of Hindley, his vendetta against the Lintons and his wickedness towards both his own son and Hareton. Such evils, however, do not give us the whole picture of Heathcliff and for this, finally, we must look at him as a man.

He has had a harsh introduction to life. Despite Nelly's attempt to boost his morale by inventing a royal parentage for him it seems most likely that he had been abandoned by his mother (probably unmarried or a prostitute) to fend for himself on the streets of Liverpool from an early age.

Emily Brontë's brother Branwell had seen such children when he was in Liverpool in 1845 and they were, unfortunately, a common sight in many big cities at the time. When he arrives at Wuthering Heights he is about seven years old; dirty, ragged and half starved, he speaks only what Nelly calls 'gibberish' – no doubt an attempt to explain himself in some foreign language. From his condition we must assume that he has had no love, nor care; he has even lacked a roof over his head. He has learned, however, to put himself first, to take what he can get while it is there and for the rest of the time to suffer passively. Both Hindley and Nelly treat him badly but he accepts their ill-nature stoically, 'hardened, perhaps,' Nelly suggests, 'to ill-treatment' (Chapter 4). However, he embraces his good fortune in being adopted into a comfortable home by making the best of it, by gaining the affection of the old man who has picked up 'the poor, fatherless child' (Chapter 4) and by reciprocating the passionate devotion of Catherine.

The death of his benefactor and the return home of Hindley are crucial factors in changing Heathcliff's life yet again, for though, economically, he is not left in the wretched state of his infant years, he is now cruelly humiliated; he suffers violence, neglect and degradation, less endurable to him now that he has tasted the good things of life than when he expected nothing from fortune but blows. It is at this point that resentment and hatred build up in the boy, tempered always by his love for Catherine for, after their adventure at Thrushcross Grange when they observe Edgar and Isabella quarrelling, he affirms to Nelly:

> I'd not exchange, for a thousand lives, my condition here, for Edgar Linton's at Thrushcross Grange – not if I might have the

> privilege of flinging Joseph off the highest gable, and painting the housefront with Hindley's blood! (Chapter 6)

This simple, almost naïve, response to emotional demands constantly grabs the reader's sympathy for Heathcliff; whilst he sees things clearly in black and white, we are repeatedly forced to mitigate our judgements recognising, behind his words and actions, reasons and motives, even justifications in an Old Testament morality that Joseph has been at least partly responsible for forcing upon the family.

In fact, before he disappears, though his verbal threats are evil, Heathcliff's actions are scarcely blameworthy; we do not regret his tussle with Skulker outside Thrushcross Grange, nor the hot apple sauce poured over the priggish Edgar; his natural instincts are not essentially evil for despite his hatred of Hindley he saves little Hareton's life. It is the apparent loss of Catherine's love that changes words to deeds when he returns after three years of bitter struggle to improve himself to find that she is already married to Edgar. Even then he has redeeming traits: he is not a drunkard like Hindley; his passionate love for Catherine has remained constant; and though he uses Hareton to revenge himself on Hindley he does not ill-treat the child. He has become, however, cunning, scheming and revengeful. Catherine sums him up to Isabella as:

> . . . an unreclaimed creature, without refinement, without cultivation; an arid wilderness of furze and whinstone . . . He's not a rough diamond – a pearl-containing oyster of a rustic; he's a fierce, pitiless, wolfish man. . . . Avarice is growing with him a besetting sin. (Chapter 10)

Heathcliff now pursues a relentless campaign of hate against the families of both Linton and Earnshaw. With Hindley he returns violence for violence, only the drunken debilitated Hindley is no match for him. He marries Isabella, as Catherine fully recognises, not out of love, but to serve his purpose of revenge. His treatment of his sickly son is diabolical yet we do not know exactly how he exerts his power over the boy; furthermore, Emily Brontë allows us so little sympathy with Linton that our repugnance for his persecutor is to some extent diminished. The forced marriage of the lively, life-loving Cathy to the wretched, whining Linton and the attempt to prevent her returning to her dying father is perhaps seen by the reader as Heathcliff's most evil act.

Yet Heathcliff's character is not entirely paradoxical; he is identified with natural forces; he loves and hates always passionately. He is not conditioned by society or civilisation; he gives a robust, natural response to every challenge, an affirmation rather than a rejection of the humanity within him.

Catherine

There is no problem about the actual identity of Catherine. She is the younger child of the Earnshaw family whose ancestors have lived in Wuthering Heights for well over two and a half centuries before her birth. Her brother Hindley is eight years older than she and another brother, the original Heathcliff, died in infancy.

We first meet Catherine before Mr Earnshaw goes on his journey to Liverpool; when he asks what she wants him to bring back for her she chooses a whip for, explains Nelly, 'she could ride any horse in the stable'. We should not ignore the symbolism of this choice, however; the whip represents domination and Catherine proves to be obstinate, self-willed and not easily subdued. When her father returns home with Heathcliff but without the whip and with Hindley's present broken to pieces, we should observe that she only grins and spits at the strange little orphan whilst Hindley, though he is fourteen years old, 'blubber[s] aloud'. As a child she has a mercurial temperament and is constantly at odds with her father. Nelly describes her at that time with affection tinged with irritation:

> ... she put all of us past our patience fifty times and oftener in a day ... Her spirits were always at high-water mark, her tongue always going – singing, laughing, and plaguing everybody who would not do the same. A wild, wick slip she was – but she had the bonniest eye, and sweetest smile, and lightest foot in the parish ...
> (Chapter 5)

Yet the adult Catherine loses her spontaneous wildness; she becomes selfish and arrogant and Nelly confesses that she 'did not like her, after her infancy was past' (Chapter 8).

We too find ourselves frequently out of sympathy with Catherine for in forsaking Heathcliff for Edgar she betrays her own heart. Her whole being is bound up in Heathcliff and his in her. It is an almost mystical relationship in which they repeatedly see themselves as facets of one another, not as two separate people. Perhaps we condemn her too easily, however, for indulging her 'poor fancy' (Chapter 15) for Edgar; first, we are judging from a kind of hindsight – we *know* that Heathcliff returns, whereas Catherine believes that he has gone for ever; secondly, she is a child of her time: her only hope of security in the future lies in marriage and Edgar offers her this security; thirdly, when she first contemplates marriage with Edgar she believes that it is also Heathcliff's only hope for a secure future. Looked at in this way we realise that, despite the seeming immorality of this idea, it has a certain logic in it and it becomes a sacrificial, rather than a selfish act.

Yet Catherine's own nature defeats her; she cannot bear to be thwarted and she has difficulty in seeing anyone's point of view but her own. Thus, she expects Edgar to be as delighted as she is at Heathcliff's return and she expects Heathcliff himself to be able to accept her loss composedly. When, inevitably, there is discord between them, Catherine flies into a rage and punishes her body for the self-inflicted anguish of her mind. The pressures placed upon her by her divided soul are too great; she is in the middle of a pregnancy and, with her physical condition grossly aggravated by her psychological state, she has what we today would understand as a nervous breakdown.

Catherine's tempestuous nature cannot reconcile itself with Edgar's calm insipidity. She wants him to react with passion to her own passionate fury. When he retires to his library and apparently withdraws from the conflict her self-love is wounded, for though she tells him, 'I don't want you, Edgar; I'm past wanting you' (Chapter 12), she nevertheless wants *him* to go on loving *her*; like all selfish people she places herself at the centre of her own universe: 'How strange!' she remarks to Nelly, 'I thought, though everybody hated and despised each other, they could not avoid loving me.'

Her death scene arouses compassion in us not for Catherine herself but for Heathcliff, for though the parting is agonising on both sides we know that he has to go on living after being lashed by her harsh and selfish words:

> You and Edgar have broken my heart, Heathcliff! . . . You have killed me – and thriven on it . . . I care nothing for your sufferings. Why shouldn't you suffer? I do! (Chapter 15)

Our knowledge of the little ghost should tell us that Catherine speaks truly; she too is to suffer; she will not be at peace until Heathcliff at last comes to her. Thus, the mystic side of her personality is reinforced at her death and we are uneasily conscious of her presence, at least to Heathcliff, throughout the rest of the novel.

Hindley

Compared with Heathcliff and Catherine, Hindley is a relatively uncomplicated character. Nevertheless, even he has his contradictory aspects: his choice of a fiddle as a present from his father suggests an artistic temperament and his tears when it is broken make him seem soft and sensitive. Yet is is a side of him we scarcely ever see again, except perhaps in his marriage. It appears that the tenderer part of him is suppressed or destroyed by the tensions which arise in the family after Heathcliff's adoption. Whilst old Mr Earnshaw is alive Hindley's attitude towards Heathcliff is bullying and violent; afterwards it is vicious and cruel, at this stage he, like Catherine, revels in his power over those weaker than himself.

Yet he loves his wife deeply and during her illness he is in desperate misery, breaking into tears before her and unable to control his emotion. Her death marks the final disintegration of his character:

> ... he grew desperate; his sorrow was of that kind that will not lament, he neither wept nor prayed – he cursed and defied – execrated God and man, and gave himself up to reckless dissipation
> (Chapter 8)

Emily Brontë had seen the results of drunken profligacy in her brother Branwell and the course which Hindley's life follows was all too familiar to her. Were Hindley's wasted artistic dreams based on the ruined hopes of Branwell?

Edgar and Isabella

We know nothing of the life of the Lintons until their fortunes are linked with those of the Earnshaws. By that time Edgar is fifteen years old and Isabella eleven, a year younger than Catherine. Though Lord David Cecil describes them as 'children of calm', we first see them in the midst of a quarrel and Heathcliff describes Isabella 'shrieking as if witches were running red-hot needles into her' (Chapter 6). Yet their passions have no substance and are easily forgotten.

In contrast to Heathcliff and the Earnshaws the Linton children are fair-haired and blue-eyed. They have been genteelly brought up and Edgar is soft-spoken and somewhat effeminate. Our first impression of him, through Nelly's eyes, is not especially favourable; he appears to be a rather pretty milksop who appeals to Catherine as the antithesis of her own person and character. Though several years older than Heathcliff he is shorter and slighter, pale-faced and weakly. He carries with him the arrogance of an upper-class youth who has lived a life of comfort and luxury, without effort or struggle on his part. Catherine's lively nature captivates him from the start. When Heathcliff leaves her, injured, in Thrushcross Grange, he peeps through the curtains before returning home; inside he sees that Catherine is the focus of attention of the Linton family and he observes Edgar's 'vacant blue eyes ... full of stupid admiration' (Chapter 6).

When she goes to Thrushcross Grange after Catherine's marriage Nelly who had displayed a mild scorn of Edgar when he was a boy, begins to think more highly of him; he is 'a kind master' (Chapter 10) and no doubt more even-tempered and easy to get on with than the inhabitants of Wuthering Heights had ever been. Yet his love for Catherine is essentially selfish and his anger with her is pettish; despite his gentleness he is unforgiving; when Catherine mocks and teases him he sulks in his library;

when Isabella defies him by marrying Heathcliff he abandons her; even Nelly finds herself depressed by his coldness to his sister.

As the novel proceeds Edgar appears to gain in stature. His sorrow at Catherine's death strikes a sympathetic chord in us and he proves to be an excellent and loving father to little Cathy. The peevishness of his responses to Catherine disappears and is replaced by a quiet and reasoned attitude towards his daughter. He entirely gains Nelly Dean's respect and Cathy loves him devotedly. He to some extent redeems his former hardness towards Isabella by immediately going to see her when she is ill and believes she is about to die; at her death he brings the ailing Linton home and is exceedingly gentle and patient with the boy's childish petulance.

Isabella resembles her brother physically but is less inhibited than he and enlivened by some sparks of spirit. Nelly describes her as 'a charming young lady . . . infantile in manners, though possessed of keen wit, keen feelings, and a keen temper, too, if irritated' (Chapter 10). Even after her disastrously foolish marriage she has the courage first to join with Hindley in locking Heathcliff out of Wuthering Heights and secondly to engage with him in bitter repartee before fleeing from the house. When she leaves for the south, however, we hear nothing more of her until the time of her death.

The second generation

The members of the second generation are not dealt with anything like so fully as their forebears. Lord David Cecil sees them as being the heirs alike of calm and storm but differing in that Hareton and Cathy are 'children of love' and Linton the 'child of hate'; certainly neither **Hareton** nor **Cathy** inherit the less desirable qualities of their parents, whereas **Linton** is an amalgam of the worst of his. Physically, Hareton is an Earnshaw with dark Earnshaw eyes and closely resembling his aunt Catherine; Linton is a Linton with nothing of Heathcliff in him; he has 'thick flaxen curls . . . slender arms . . . small fingers . . . and . . . great blue eyes' (Chapter 20); Cathy, being both Earnshaw and Linton has, like Hareton, the dark Earnshaw eyes but the 'fair skin and small features, and yellow curling hair' of the Lintons (Chapter 18).

With calmer characters as protagonists, the second part of the book is less turbulent than the first. Cathy, though self-willed like her mother, is more affectionate and more considerate and she has no bosom companion like Heathcliff with whom to indulge in wild escapades. Nevertheless, she brings her own misery upon herself by disobeying her father and defying Nelly in order to visit her cousin Linton at Wuthering Heights. Having had nothing to thwart her in childhood, she is bold and fearless and stands up to Heathcliff with remarkable resilience. Her marriage to Linton, however foolish it may seem, is entered into readily on her part for she believes that he both loves her and needs her. She is too inexperienced to recognise his selfishness or Heathcliff's cruelty and she throws her warmth and affection away on the beautiful and romantically fragile boy. Linton does not deserve her love. Ailing and sickly, he is also self-absorbed and self-centred. In mitigation, however, we should remember his dire state of health, the constant pain and distress he suffers and the miserable isolation he endures in Wuthering Heights. It is difficult to condemn entirely his treachery to Cathy because he is clearly afraid for his life and physically and morally he is too weak to stand up to this fear.

Cathy's marriage to Linton is a vicarious atonement for the sin of her mother's rejection of Heathcliff and marriage to Edgar. Like Heathcliff, Cathy can achieve peace only through suffering. Thus she moves through her hopeless marriage to Linton towards harmony in her second marriage to Hareton Earnshaw. Hareton is little more than a rough sketch of a character. The country boor who turns out to have a heart of gold, his transformation into the loved and loving friend of Cathy is necessary to the resolution of the plot, though not entirely convincing. His 'startling likeness to Catherine' (Chapter 33) is perhaps his most significant aspect; for Heathcliff he becomes simultaneously the ghostly *alter ego* of both Catherine and Heathcliff himself; his destruction would be Heathcliff's final victory and final defeat. Thus, the marriage of Cathy and Hareton is a substitute for the marriage which never took place between Catherine and Heathcliff; Hareton who is Heathcliff's spiritual heir paves the way through his own happiness for the spiritual happiness of Heathcliff with Catherine.

The narrators

Lockwood and **Nelly Dean** are the principal narrators, the former giving an outside view of the story, the latter offering us insights from a subjective observer closely involved with a number of the protagonists. Lockwood can scarcely be considered as a rounded character. We know little about his background and education, though, like the Lintons, he is soft, a man of sentimental impulses but not of passion. He appears to see himself as a romantic hero and the only incident of his past life he chooses to tell us is that of his encounter at the seaside the previous year with 'a most fascinating creature, a real goddess' (Chapter 1), an encounter which he was afraid to allow to develop into reality. We should remember this during his narration, for he is not a man who easily understands the characters of others and his first judgement of Heathcliff is certainly faulty. For him, Nelly's tale is one in which he participates in his own imagination and at a distance; he ends his account of the first part, i.e. Chapters 1–31 with the words:

> What a realization of something more romantic than a fairy tale it would have been for Mrs Linton Heathcliff, had she and I struck up an attachment ... and migrated together, into the stirring atmosphere of the town!

Lockwood returns to Thrushcross Grange on impulse and is thus enabled to hear the end of Nelly's tale. The oddly romantic streak in him still gives him a part in the story; when he sees Cathy and Hareton together he takes on the role of jealous lover biting his lip in spite 'at having thrown away the chance [he] might have had' (Chapter 32). It is a role we do not recognise him in!

Nelly, on the other hand, is far more down to earth. Hindley's age, she has been brought up with the Earnshaw children as something between older sister and nurse; she later becomes housekeeper, first at Wuthering Heights and then at Thrushcross Grange. By her own account she is self-educated; a 'poor man's daughter' (Chapter 7). She is an avid reader and has read most of the books in the library at the Grange. Though she appears to be entirely dependent on the families for whom she works she is not an especially reliable servant. Time and again she betrays the trust her masters have in her: she fails to fulfil Mr Earnshaw's orders on the night when Heathcliff is first brought to Wuthering Heights (Chapter 4); she connives with Catherine to frustrate Hindley's punishment of Heathcliff at the Christmas feast of 1777 (Chapter 7); and she constantly deceives Edgar, first in her dealings with Heathcliff and Catherine and later by concealing Cathy's visits to Wuthering Heights. Yet, apart from her neglect of the newly-arrived Heathcliff, her actions are generally prompted by kindness and humanity or by the desire to avoid trouble for Edgar Linton. Though it is possible to question her judgement, her motives are not suspect. She has the interests of her masters at heart; she alone is the confidante of the principals in the tale; in turn, Catherine, Cathy and Heathcliff confide in her. By the end of the book she has established herself as a typical old family retainer.

4.2 STYLE AND LANGUAGE

Despite the very exact chronology of *Wuthering Heights* the novel is, paradoxically, timeless in essence and this is as much owing to its style and language as to its characters and plot. The conversational tone and fairy-story element are as alive today as they were when Emily Brontë wrote the novel and we should remember that its setting was already some fifty years back from her own time. Though it is a raconteur's tale, however, it is highly poetic and rich in linguistic devices, ranging from the simple similes of Nelly's language to the sustained imagery of the novel as a whole.

Except, perhaps, for Joseph's dialect, the vocabulary presents few difficulties and certainly none that a good concise dictionary cannot solve. Even Joseph should not cause us too many problems for we are given a fairly precise phonetic transcription of his speech; read out phonetically it gives excellently the sense of what he is saying, even to someone quite unacquainted with the dialect itself. It is probable, of course, that most of the characters from the Heights, if not from the Grange, would have spoken with a strong Yorkshire accent, and indeed, Hareton progresses during the novel from a rough country vernacular to something more refined. One of the principal achievements of Joseph's dialect is that it succeeds in turning him into a caricature rather than a character – a comic rustic rather than a spiteful religious fanatic. The other protagonists speak mainly a sort of standard English because Emily Brontë wants us to take them seriously.

The various narrators have the gift of recounting dialogue as in the actual words of the characters concerned. Thus Lockwood presents Nelly's story as she tells it and Nelly reproduces the actual words of Catherine, Heathcliff and the rest; likewise both Lockwood and Nelly are adept at mimicking Joseph. The most noticeable change in style when Nelly first takes over the narration in Chapter 4 is the sudden proliferation of similes and metaphors. Lockwood is very observant and has excellent descriptive powers but Nelly's language is more picturesque. She constantly snatches similes from her own country environment, particularly from animal life: 'like an unfledged dunnock . . . uncomplaining as a lamb' (Chapter 4), 'mute as mice' (Chapter 6), but sometimes from other aspects of the country: 'Rough as a saw-edge . . . hard as whinstone' (Chapter 4) or even from outside her own immediate knowledge: 'bright as diamonds . . . rude as savages' (Chapter 6). She has generally a very vivid turn of phrase, giving us again and again memorable word pictures to reinforce her ideas; so when Heathcliff saves Hareton from falling to his death she comments:

> A miser who has parted with a lucky lottery ticket for five shillings, and finds next day he has lost in the bargain five thousand pounds, could not show a blanker countenance than he did on beholding the figure of Mr Earnshaw above. (Chapter 9)

Both Catherine and Heathcliff share Nelly's gift for graphic language; thus, Catherine can put clearly her relative feelings for Edgar and Heathcliff by comparison with the natural landscape around her:

> My love for Linton is like the foliage in the woods. Time will change it, I'm well aware, as winter changes the trees. My love

for Heathcliff resembles the eternal rocks beneath – a source of little visible delight, but necessary. (Chapter 9)

Or Heathcliff can compare Hindley's son with his own in striking metaphors, 'one is gold put to the use of paving-stones; and the other is tin polished to ape a service of silver' (Chapter 21).

Interspersed with these vivid pictures are the simple phrases which suggest the rhythm of country life. Many of the chapters open, for instance, with a 'time-pointer': 'On the morning of a fine June day ... ' (Chapter 8); 'About twelve o'clock, that night ... ' (Chapter 16); 'That Friday made the last of our fine days, for a month' (Chapter 17); 'Summer drew to an end, and early Autumn' (Chapter 22); 'These things happened last winter' (Chapter 25); 'Summer was already past its prime' (Chapter 26). So the pattern of continuing life in its ordinary phases is imposed upon the strangeness and violence of the story being told and the language enables us to accept them side by side.

The other major aspect of style which must be considered is the extraordinarily powerful use of sustained imagery. Apart from the two houses, the most significant is the group of interrelated images based on windows, doors, locks and keys. First, they reflect an idea that crops up innumerable times during the novel, the 'inside-outside' theme; on a simple level windows frame, for a character looking through them, the scene on the other side; for instance, in Chapter 2, Lockwood within Wuthering Heights comments:

> I approached a window to examine the weather.
> A sorrowful sight I saw; dark night coming down prematurely, and sky and hills mingled in one bitter whirl of wind and suffocating snow.

And in Chapter 6 Heathcliff and Catherine look into Thrushcross Grange from outside the drawing-room window. The contrast of inside and outside scenes, however, is more often emphasised by the longing to pass from one side to the other of a window or door; a separation is imaged which is never easily overcome by the mere removal of the physical barrier: in Chapter 3 Lockwood's little ghost is outside, longing to come in; in Chapter 12 Catherine, sick and unhappy at Thrushcross Grange, is inside, longing to get out. Locked doors, stapled windows, keys intensify the sense of separation; life for the inhabitants of the two houses is a constant struggle for personal freedom, frustrated by the wills of others and by the restraints of locks and keys: in Chapter 7 Heathcliff is locked in his room in the garret; in Chapter 11, during the quarrel between Edgar and Heathcliff, Catherine locks the kitchen door and throws the key in the fire; Heathcliff keeps Isabella in his 'custody' at Wuthering Heights (Chapter 14) and he kidnaps and locks up both Nelly and Catherine (Chapter 27).

There are so many examples of this kind of imagery in the novel that it would be impossible to cite them all here; readers should look for them themselves and try to understand their purpose when they appear. Throughout the first thirty-one chapters of the novel the imagery keeps us continuously aware of the restrictive nature of the lives of the protagonists. The last three chapters presage the change which takes place at the end. Constraints are no longer apparent. When Lockwood arrives again at Wuthering Heights after his absence in London doors and windows are open; finally, in Catherine's old bedroom, Heathcliff dies beside the open window through which, we have no doubt, his spirit escapes to join with Catherine's on the moors. Certainly, not long before her death, Catherine complains of being 'enclosed' in the 'shattered prison' of her physical body (Chapter 15). If their bodies are indeed prisons, then death enfranchises them. Again, it is a peculiarly religious concept.

Besides the similes referred to above, animals are used more extensively in the novel, generally to indicate something about the uncivilised or brutish side of man. The numerous dogs, very real beasts though they are, image violence and whenever dogs are present they are shown savaging someone or being themselves savaged. The first such incident occurs in Chapter 1 when Lockwood is unfortunate enough to make faces at the dogs and is set on by them for his pains; in the following chapter he is again attacked, this time by Gnasher and Wolf at the bidding of Joseph. Catherine, in Chapter 6, is bitten by the Linton's bulldog and Cathy and her dogs are attacked by the dogs from Wuthering Heights in Chapter 18. Dogs themselves, however, suffer cruelly from human violence; Isabella and Edgar quarrel spitefully, almost pulling their little dog to pieces (Chapter 6); Heathcliff, in the act of eloping with Isabella, hangs her spaniel Fanny from a bridle hook in the wall of the Grange park (Chapter 12); and little Hareton hangs a litter of puppies in the doorway of Wuthering Heights in Chapter 17. The one time when Hareton attempts to reverse the trend by giving Cathy a terrier puppy as a peace-offering, his gift is rejected (Chapter 18).

Attention has already been drawn to the significance of eyes in the novel but references to teeth also occur frequently; see, for instance, Chapter 17 where Heathcliff is described as having 'sharp cannibal teeth', Joseph is called a 'toothless hound' and Isabella is shaken till her 'teeth rattled'; discover others for yourselves. Likewise, from the moment when Lockwood rubs the little ghost's wrist across the broken glass of the window pane, blood is an important motif; its association with violence emphasises the idea of life in the raw as it is constantly seen at Wuthering Heights. Its final appearance – or non-appearance – in the novel at Heathcliff's death, 'no blood trickled from the broken skin' (Chapter 34), would thus appear to point to Heathcliff's final transformation from his stormy life on earth to the peace of the spirit world.

As you read, consider the significance of dreams and the presentation of 'other worlds' through the imaginations particularly of Catherine and Heathcliff; observe the images of dissolution, such as Catherine's 'Every Linton on the face of the earth might melt into nothing, before I could consent to forsake Heathcliff!' (Chapter 9). Examine the uses of the images of hot and cold, generally used to distinguish Heathcliff and Edgar respectively:

> Whatever our souls are made of, his and mine are the same, and Linton's is as different as a moonbeam from lightning, or frost from fire. (Chapter 9)

Notice how often we are given descriptions of the weather and ask yourself to what extent snow or rain or clear sunny days suggest the direction the story is taking. Look, too, at the frequent references to knives or pistols and try to assess their part in the story, not only as weapons but as constant motifs. Finally, see if you can yourself find other images or motifs which appear in the novel and to which no reference has been made above.

5 SPECIMEN PASSAGE AND COMMENTARY

This chapter is entirely devoted to a detailed critical examination of a passage from Chapter 3 of *Wuthering Heights*.

5.1 SPECIMEN PASSAGE

This time, I remembered I was lying in the oak closet, and I heard distinctly the gusty wind, and the driving of the snow; I heard, also, the fir-bough repeat its teasing sound, and ascribed it to the right cause; but it annoyed me so much, that I resolved to silence it, if possible; and, I thought, I rose and endeavoured to unhasp the casement. The hook was soldered into the staple, a circumstance observed by me when awake, but forgotten.

'I must stop it, nevertheless!' I muttered, knocking my knuckles through the glass, and stretching an arm out to seize the importunate branch: instead of which, my fingers closed on the fingers of a little ice-cold hand!

The intense horror of nightmare came over me; I tried to draw back my arm, but the hand clung to it, and a most melancholy voice sobbed,

'Let me in – let me in!'

'Who are you?' I asked, struggling, meanwhile, to disengage myself.

'Catherine Linton,' it replied shiveringly (why did I think of *Linton*? I had read *Earnshaw* twenty times for Linton), 'I'm come home, I'd lost my way on the moor!'

As it spoke, I discerned, obscurely, a child's face looking through the window – terror made me cruel; and, finding it useless to attempt shaking the creature off, I pulled its wrist on to the broken pane, and rubbed it to and fro till the blood ran down and soaked the bed-clothes; still it wailed, 'Let me in!' and maintained its tenacious gripe, almost maddening me with fear.

'How can I!' I said at length. 'Let *me* go, if you want me to let you in!'

The fingers relaxed, I snatched mine through the hole, hurriedly piled the books up in a pyramid against it, and stopped my ears to exclude the lamentable prayer.

I seemed to keep them closed above a quarter of an hour, yet, the instant I listened, again, there was the doleful cry moaning on!

'Begone!' I shouted, 'I'll never let you in, not if you beg for twenty years.'

'It's twenty years,' mourned the voice, 'twenty years, I've been a waif for twenty years!'

5.2 COMMENTARY

In this passage Lockwood reports the second of the nightmares he experiences whilst he is concealed in the oak closet where Catherine Earnshaw had slept as a child. Unable to sleep at first, he had been reading Catherine's diary from some twenty-five years earlier; this was written on every empty page and blank scrap of paper in the printed books on her window sill. Whilst Lockwood's first nightmare was sparked off by the title-page of an actual printed book, this second nightmare seems to have its origin in the vivid impression left on his mind by the hand-written diary and the names scrawled on the window sill, though his own experiences of the preceding day are also significant.

Disconcertingly, the dream begins in what appears to be the wakefulness of reality, for the gusty wind and driving snow, described in somewhat similar terms in the previous chapter, are the reasons for Lockwood being marooned overnight in Wuthering Heights. The changes in the weather are a significant feature throughout the novel. Early in the first chapter Lockwood refers to the bleak position of Wuthering Heights and explains that 'wuthering' is a provincial term to describe the storm wind blowing across the moor. As the story progresses, the weather appears to be in tune with the events recorded; for instance, the October evening when Mr Earnshaw dies is wild and stormy (Chapter 5), the summer night that Heathcliff disappears is threatening with thunder and a violent storm ensues (Chapter 9), whilst during the period when Heathcliff is approaching death 'the weather was sweet and warm' (Chapter 34).

The window which features so centrally here is a recurrent motif in the novel; it serves as a separator: the world outside the window and the world within are constantly contrasted with each other. Already in the previous chapter Lockwood has looked from the warmth and security of Wuthering Heights out on the prematurely dark night with the whirling wind and snow. Now, however, the window is given more detailed attention. Outside is one of the fir trees he had observed when he first approached the house; it is the very fir tree down which Cathy climbs in Chapter 28 in order to make good her escape from the Heights. The window, however, is now fixed, the hook 'soldered into the staple' – a precursor of the many references to locked doors and windows. When we reach Chapter 28 we shall realise that at that point, only a few weeks earlier, in September 1801, the window opens in normal fashion; we can only assume that Heathcliff, angry at Cathy's escape, belatedly makes the window secure. It is he too who wrenches the window open again after Lockwood's nightmare. A few months later, in the final chapter of the book, Heathcliff dies beside this same window which he has opened and left flapping to and fro in the wind. The fact that Nelly then hasps the window hardly matters, for Catherine and Heathcliff are no longer separated.

The 'inside-outside' theme is recalled a number of times throughout the novel. A few chapters further on Catherine and Heathcliff find themselves outside the window of Thrushcross Grange, looking in at the elegantly splendid drawing-room where Isabella and Edgar are quarrelling over a pet dog. It is the last time that Catherine and Heathcliff are together in unsullied harmony; when Catherine passes from one side to the other of that window, there is an end to all their happiness.

More hauntingly reminiscent of this nightmare scene, however, are three other incidents which take place later in the novel. The first occurs at Thrushcross Grange when Catherine is taken ill after the violent quarrel between Edgar and Heathcliff following the latter's surreptitious embracing of Isabella (Chapter 12). Catherine wilfully starves herself and works herself up into an emotionally disturbed state. At the height of her fever she dreams that she is in her own room at Wuthering Heights; she imagines that she hears the 'wind sounding in the firs by the lattice' and this, together with the cold blast which sweeps through the room when Nelly briefly opens the window, reminds us of the blizzard on the night of Lockwood's nightmare. The ghostly child is directly recalled to our attention by Nelly's words, 'our fiery Catherine was no better than a wailing child'. Here is the wailing Catherine Linton of the nightmare, longing to be inside the panelled room at Wuthering Heights.

Both the other incidents take place at the Heights itself. The night following Catherine's funeral Hindley and Isabella lock Heathcliff out of Wuthering Heights (Chapter 17). Again it is a night with 'wild snow blowing outside and a moaning wind'; Heathcliff, like the little ghost, wants to come inside. Just as Lockwood breaks the window and commits an act of cruelty which results in the bedclothes being soaked with blood, so Heathcliff breaks the window and commits an act of violence against Hindley who is left lying in a pool of blood. The second incident occurs at Heathcliff's death (already referred to above, so many interwoven threads cross and recross to link parts of the book together). This scene is a complete contrast, yet both the setting and the language unerringly recall Lockwood's nightmare. Now the window is open; there is no snow but the rain has poured down in the night and the bedclothes are soaked with rain, not with blood; the absence of blood is emphasised for, though Heathcliff's hand lying on the sill is grazed, 'no blood trickled from the broken skin'. Lockwood's little ghost is more alive than Heathcliff for it is the blood from her wrist which runs down and soaks the bedclothes.

The ghost itself and the words 'twenty years', which occur in our extract three times, also draw their significance from a later (though chronologically earlier) event in the book - the death of Catherine, reported in Chapters 15 and 16. In the last, passionate, agonising meeting between Catherine and Heathcliff she accuses him of not caring that she is about to die; she asserts that he will easily forget her, that 'twenty years hence' he will look upon her grave and remember that he 'loved her long ago'. Tantalisingly for the reader, it is not twenty years since Catherine's death, for she died in 1784 and it is now 1801. For the appearance of the ghost, Heathcliff must be held responsible! When he learns of Catherine's death he prays that she may haunt him: 'ghosts *have* wandered on earth. Be with me always - take any form - drive me mad!' The nightmare shows Catherine's ghost both wandering on earth and driving him mad for, though she is perfectly visible to Lockwood, Heathcliff, despite his tormented plea, cannot see her.

The theme of the supernatural occurs repeatedly in the book. The vocabulary of the supernatural is especially prominent; already the early chapters of the novel have yielded such words as 'magically . . . ministering angel . . . beneficent fairy . . . little witch'; Cathy has threatened Joseph with the 'Black Art' and, when she fears that Lockwood may become lost and die on the bleak moor she tells Hareton that she hopes 'his ghost will haunt you'. Throughout the novel the tension is kept high by the feeling of unease aroused by references to 'heaven . . . hell . . . devil . . . Satan . . . fiend . . . ghosts . . . goblin . . . ghoul . . . vampire' and, even at the end, the phrasing of Lockwood's last sentence encourages us to believe rather than disbelieve the stories that are told about Catherine and Heathcliff walking the moors together. Why does he linger, watch and listen if he thinks there is nothing to watch and listen?

Lockwood's question, ' . . . why did I think of *Linton*?' perhaps deserves comment. The names 'Heathcliff' and 'Earnshaw' he had already met with in the persons of Heathcliff himself and Hareton Earnshaw;

Cathy too is 'Mrs Heathcliff'. 'Linton' completes the triangle; it is the one name Lockwood cannot at that time connect with any actual living being. Significantly, it is, of course, the true designation of the ghost, though not of the child; he imagines a child because of the 'unformed, childish hand' he had been reading but, if the ghost has any reality, it is the ghost of the Catherine who had married Edgar Linton and thus separated herself from Heathcliff.

This extract is part of the outer narrative framework of the novel; the 'I' is Lockwood who is the principal narrator, within whose narration are contained the narrations of a number of other characters. Already Catherine's diary has made its contribution but Ellen Dean who tells most of the story is yet to appear. Each of the narratives is told in the voice of the particular narrator so that here we can observe Lockwood's careful attention to detail and his meticulous powers of observation. There is an absence, however, of the lively similes which colour Nelly's narration.

The whole sequence of events when Lockwood is in the panelled closet is seminal to the novel and study of this second nightmare is especially rewarding.

6 CRITICAL APPRAISALS

For details of reviews and other comments cited in this section see the following books: Emily Brontë, *Wuthering Heights*, ed. David Daiches; *Emily Brontë: Wuthering Heights* and *The Brontës: The Critical Heritage* both edited by Miriam Allott

The first critics of *Wuthering Heights* were Emily's sisters, Charlotte and Anne, who heard the novel, or at least part of it, 'read in manuscript'. Their response was one of awe and even of terror at the presentation of characters whose natures were so 'relentless and implacable . . . so lost and fallen'. At the same time they recognised its extraordinary power and were ready enough to send it for publication together with their own first novels. When it was published in a three-volume edition with Anne's *Agnes Grey* in December 1847 it was perhaps not surprising that most of the reviews, whilst not ignoring *Agnes Grey*, gave considerably greater attention to *Wuthering Heights*.

6.1 CONTEMPORARY CRITICISM

It is not infrequently suggested that the reception of *Wuthering Heights* in 1847-8 was unfavourable, even hostile; though this is true to some extent, it is not universally true. The view has probably been given currency by some comments which appeared in Charlotte Brontë's 'Biographical Notice of Ellis and Acton Bell' which was published together with a critical Preface in the 1850 edition of *Wuthering Heights and Agnes Grey*. There she asserts, 'Critics failed to do them justice. The immature but very real powers revealed in *Wuthering Heights* were scarcely recognised.' Yet Charlotte would undoubtedly have read the five reviews which were found in Emily's desk after her death and of these, one, anonymous and with its origin still unidentified, is both perceptive and commendatory; it displays considerable sensitivity in its understanding of, and sympathetic approach to, both the setting and the characters of the novel. Its simple critical stance recognises the significance of the two houses and of the two opposing families, though it fails to remark upon the narrative skill and the highly evocative language of the novel.

There is little doubt that *Wuthering Heights* suffered from being published a few months after *Jane Eyre*. First, many readers insisted on believing, despite avowals to the contrary, that the two novels were written by the same hand and that *Wuthering Heights* was an earlier and less mature novel; secondly, *Jane Eyre* is more accessible on a first reading, its protagonists are more conventionally romantic and its plot more comprehensible in human terms. Consequently, there was, in many of the reviews, a general tendency to compare *Wuthering Heights* unfavourably with *Jane Eyre*. On the other hand, the very existence of Charlotte's novel drew attention to that of her sister and kept it in the public eye.

The principal criticisms arose perhaps from the impossibility of reading several times, and browsing over, a novel that had to be reviewed for a printer's deadline. The reviewer in *The Examiner* for 8 January 1848, for instance, saw the story as confused and found it difficult to 'set [the incidents] forth in chronological order'; in the *Britannia* for 15 January 1848 the novel was said to be 'in parts very unskilfully constructed'; on 22 January 1848 the *Atlas* reviewer called it 'a strange, inartistic story'. Yet the chronology is carefully planned, the multiple narration cunningly contrived and these, together with the pattern of symbols and linguistic motifs, give the novel an artistic wholeness rarely equalled in the nineteenth century.

Another problem that beset the early reviewers was that the novel seemed to have no 'moral' or contain no 'message'; several of them sought the 'purpose' behind the book and concluded that there was none. The most common attack, however, was on the tone and language of the novel. The *Spectator* for 18 December 1847 claimed that the 'incidents are too coarse and disagreeable to be attractive'; the *American Review* for June 1848 also described the novel as 'coarse', maintaining that 'there is such a general roughness and savageness in the soliloquies and dialogues here given as never should be found in a work of art'; several months later, in October 1848, the reviewer for the *North American Review* was equally scathing, asserting that the author of the novel (whom he carelessly assumed to be Acton Bell, i.e. Anne!), 'details all the ingenuities of animal malignity, and exhausts the whole rhetoric of stupid blasphemy'. Such criticisms, though ill-founded, are perhaps comprehensible in the light of nineteenth-century prudery in both Britain and the United States, though it is difficult today to see what all the fuss was about.

The harsher criticism of the book, however, was tempered by a recognition, in practically every review, of the power of the novel. Even the anger which Heathcliff seemed to evoke in the hearts of several of the reviewers is sufficient evidence of this but it was, in fact, repeatedly stated more explicitly:

> . . . the delineation is forcible and truthful.
>
> *(Spectator*, 18 December 1847)

> . . . much power and cleverness . . .
>
> (*Athenaeum* , 25 December 1847)

> It is not without evidences of considerable power . . .
>
> (*Examiner*, 8 January 1848)

> He displays considerable power in his creations . . . there is singular power in his portraiture of strong passion.
>
> (*Britannia*, 15 January 1848)

> There seems to us great power in this book . . .
>
> (*Douglas Jerrold's Weekly Newspaper*, 15 January 1848)

> There are evidences in every chapter of a sort of rugged power . . .
>
> (*Atlas*, 22 January 1848)

> This novel contains, undoubtedly powerful writing. . .
>
> (*Tait's Edinburgh Magazine*, February 1848)

> . . . the immense power, of the book, - a rough, shaggy, uncouth power . . .
>
> (*Literary World*, April 1848)

> . . . a coarse, original, powerful book.
>
> (*American Review*, June 1848)

This unanimity of response is particularly striking, of course, when such comments are isolated from the rest of what was said in the various reviews, as they are above; it does, however, suggest that the impact of the novel, even in those early months, was considerable, though the reviewers were often at a loss to show in detail what had impressed them.

6.2 TWENTIETH-CENTURY CRITICISM

Today, *Wuthering Heights* is firmly established as one of the great novels of the nineteenth century. An enormous number of critical articles and books has been devoted to it and it has attracted a wide variety of inter-pretations. In the space available it is impossible to make a representative selection of significant twentieth-century criticism and it may seem invidious to choose the comments of only one or two critics. However, printed below are a couple of extracts from what is perhaps the best known critique on *Wuthering Heights*, that by Lord David Cecil, published in 1934. It is so frequently quoted that any student of the novel should be aware of it; yet it is by no means a complete and final interpretation and, in order that you may realise that there are other views, it is followed by two shorter pieces, one from Miriam Allott's essay 'The Rejection of Heathcliff' and the second from David Daiches' Introduction to the Penguin English Library edition of *Wuthering Heights*, both of which suggest insufficiencies in Cecil's approach.

From Lord David Cecil

The setting is a microcosm of the universal scheme as Emily Brontë conceived it. On the one hand, we have Wuthering Heights, the land of storm; high on the barren moorland, naked to the shock of the elements, the natural home of the Earnshaw family, fiery, untamed children of the storm. On the other, sheltered in the leafy valley below, stands, Thrushcross Grange, the appropriate home of the children of calm, the gentle, passive timid Lintons. Together each group, following its own nature in its own sphere, combines to compose a cosmic harmony. It is the destruction and re-establishment of this harmony which is the theme of the story. It opens with the arrival at Wuthering Heights of an extraneous element – Heathcliff. He, too, is a child of the storm; and the affinity between him and Catherine Earnshaw makes them fall in love with each other. But since he is an extraneous element, he is a source of discord, inevitably disrupting the working of the natural order. He drives the father, Earnshaw, into conflict with the son, Hindley, and as a result Hindley into conflict with himself, Heathcliff. The order is still further dislocated by Catherine, who is seduced into uniting herself in an 'unnatural' marriage with Linton, the child of calm. The shock of her infidelity and Hindley's ill-treatment of him now, in its turn, disturbs the natural harmony of Heathcliff's nature, and turns him from an alien element in the established order, into a force active for its destruction. He is not therefore, as usually supposed, a wicked man voluntarily yielding to his wicked impulses. Like all Emily Brontë's characters, he is a manifestation of natural forces acting involuntarily under the pressure of his own nature. But he is a natural force which has been frustrated of its natural outlet, so that it inevitably becomes destructive; like a mountain torrent diverted from its channel, which flows out on the surrounding country, laying waste whatever may happen to lie in its way. Nor can it stop doing so, until the obstacles which kept it from its natural channel are removed.

From Miriam Allott

... the conclusions drawn by Cecil from his study of the novel ... are not self-evident conclusions. It is true that if they are accepted as self-evident, an interpretation of *Wuthering Heights* can be made which does justice to many elements of Emily Brontë's art, but at the same time the pattern of the novel suffers distortion, and much has to be overlooked. Again, the conclusions are in themselves extraordinary. If the storm and calm principles are neither conflicting nor destructive, if the discords are only transitory, and if the final harmony is the re-establishment of an original equilibrium, surely *Wuthering Heights* should leave us feeling less troubled and haunted than in fact it does?

Indeed the whole structure of the novel suggests a deeper and more compulsive concern with the elements of 'storm' than this reading allows for.

From David Daiches

This [i.e. David Cecil's view] is both neat and ingenious, but it leaves out too much and does not adequately account either for the novel's power or for the symbolic elements that operate in it. Why should the fatuous Lockwood be visited by the ghost of the dead Catherine and why should he give way to a sadistic impulse to rub the child's wrist across the broken glass of the window pane (the cruellest of many cruel images in the book)? What is the meaning of the recurring sadism in the story? What, if any, kind of morality is involved? What is the imagination really doing in this disturbingly violent tale?

REVISION QUESTIONS

1. Examine the incident in which Catherine and Heathcliff go to Thrushcross Grange and are attacked by the bulldog. Discuss its significance to the novel as a whole.

2. What does Emily Brontë achieve by giving the reader two accounts of the incident in which Isabella and Hindley lock Heathcliff out of Wuthering Heights?

3. Consider the significance of *either* dreams *or* letters in the novel.

4. Why do you think Emily Brontë chose Lockwood as her principal narrator?

5. Consider the use of multiple narration in the novel.

6. What advantages are there in beginning the story of *Wuthering Heights* 'in medias res'?

7. Discuss the part played in the novel by *either* Joseph *or* Isabella *or* Zillah.

8. Do you see Heathcliff as villain or hero?

9. Try to assess the signifance of the relationship between Heathcliff and Hareton.

10. Examine the 'fairy-tale' elements of *Wuthering Heights*. What is their value to the novel?

11. Describe Wuthering Heights and Thrushcross Grange as fully as you can, making use of all the details given to you throughout the novel.

12. Compare and contrast the two Catherines.

13. Discuss what seems to you to be the principal theme of the novel.

14. What do you think is the significance of the many incidents in the novel concerned with dogs?

15. Discuss the significance of doors and windows in the novel.

16. Nelly Dean has been described as 'the ideal servant'. Is she?

17. How significant do you consider the frequent references to the weather?

18. Examine in detail the paragraph in Chapter 9 beginning ' "It is not," retorted she' and try to suggest what light it throws on our understanding of Catherine, Heathcliff and Edgar Linton.

19. Examine in detail the opening eight paragraphs of Chapter 11 (down to ' . . .not altered greatly since I left him, ten months since') and use them as a starting-point for commenting on Emily Brontë's style and language.

20. Examine in detail Heathcliff's explanation to Nelly in Chapter 33 of his reasons for abandoning his course of revenge (' "It is a poor conclusion, is it not" he observed . . .I can give them no attention any more') and consider its significance in our understanding of the plot.

FURTHER READING

Text

A good text to use is that in the Penguin English Library, edited by David Daiches (1965). It is essentially the text of the 1847 edition with the misprints corrected. Besides the Introduction and Notes by Daiches it contains Charlotte Brontë's 'Biographical Notice of Ellis and Acton Bell' and her Preface to the 1850 edition of *Wuthering Heights*.

Other books to read which may help to throw light on 'Wuthering Heights' or its author.:

Brontë, Charlotte, *Jane Eyre* (1847), ed. Q. D. Leavis, Penguin English Library (Penguin Books, 1966). *Shirley* (1849), eds. A. and J. Hook, Penguin English Library (Penguin Books, 1974).

Brontë, Emily, *Complete Poems*, ed. C. W. Hatfield (Columbia University Press, 1941).

Gaskell, Elizabeth, *The Life of Charlotte Brontë* (1857), ed. A. Shelton, Penguin English Library (Penguin Books, 1975).

Biography

Gérin, Winifred, *Emily Brontë: A Biography* (Clarendon Press, 1971).

Criticism

Allot, Miriam (ed.), *Emily Brontë: Wuthering Heights*, Casebook Series (Macmillan, 1970).

(ed.), *The Brontës: The Critical Heritage* (Routledge and Kegan Paul, 1974).

Cecil, Lord David, 'Emily Brontë and *Wuthering Heights*' in *Early Victorian Novelists* (1934), (repr. Penguin Books, 1948; out of print).

Goodridge, Frank. *Emily Brontë: Wuthering Heights*, Studies in English Literature No. 20 (Edward Arnold, 1964).

S., C.P. (i.e. C. P. Sanger). *The Structure of Wuthering Heights*, Hogarth Essays No 19 (L. and V. Woolf, 1926; out of print).